MW01264594

DIVINE Healing

JIMMY SWAGGART

JIMMY SWAGGART MINISTRIES
P.O. Box 262550 | Baton Rouge, Louisiana 70826-2550
www.jsm.org

ISBN 978-1-941403-60-0

09-139 | COPYRIGHT © 2019 Jimmy Swaggart Ministries®

19 20 21 22 23 24 25 26 27 28/ CM / 10 9 8 7 6 5 4 3 2 1

All rights reserved. Printed and bound in U.S.A.

No part of this publication may be reproduced in any form or
by any means without the publisher's prior written permission.

TABLE OF CONTENTS

DIVINE *Healing*

INTRODUCTION

INTRODUCTION

I HOPE THE READER will take the time to peruse this introduction to the book *Divine Healing*. It will set the stage, I think, for that which will be said:

- Does the Lord still heal the sick? At times He does.
- Are we saying that the Lord doesn't always heal in answer to prayer? That's exactly what we are saying.
- Why doesn't He always heal, that is, if it's biblical to be healed at all? While it is always the will of God to heal the sick, it's not always His wisdom.
- Is it always a lack of faith? Sometimes it is, and sometimes it isn't.
- We must understand that the entirety of humanity, even believers, still lives under the shadow of the fall. This means that the physical body ages and finally wears out. At the present time, there is nothing that can be done about that.
- Will the Lord at times heal unsaved people? Yes, at times He will, but He is under no obligation to do so.

- Does it hinder one's faith to see a doctor or to take medicine? No! In fact, in the coming kingdom age, when our Lord will rule and reign on this earth personally, medicine will be dispensed all over the world (Ezek. 47:12).

- Does the Lord use other means at times to heal, such as doctors, medicine, etc.? Yes, He does.

- Is all sickness caused by demon spirits all of the time? No. Sickness is caused by a multitude of things; however, demon spirits most definitely can cause sickness at times.

- Have you ever personally been healed? Yes, I have. Actually, I will begin this book by giving the testimony of the time that the Lord miraculously and gloriously healed me.

- Do you personally pray for the sick? Yes, I do.

O Thou God of my salvation,
My Redeemer from all sin;
Moved by Thy divine compassion,
Who has died my heart to win,
I will praise Thee, I will praise Thee;
Where shall I Thy praise begin?
I will praise Thee, I will praise Thee;
Where shall I Thy praise begin?

Though unseen, I love the Saviour;
He hath brought salvation near;
Manifests His pardoning favor;
And when Jesus does appear;
Soul and body, soul and body
Shall His glorious image bear.
Soul and body, soul and body
Shall His glorious image bear.

While the angel choirs are crying,
"Glory to the great I Am,"
I with them will still be vying—
Glory, glory to the Lamb!
O how precious, O how precious
Is the sound of Jesus' name!
O how precious, O how precious
Is the sound of Jesus' name!

Angels now are hovering 'round us,
Unperceived amid the throng:
Wondering at the love that crowned us,
Glad to join the holy song:
Hallelujah, Hallelujah,
Love and praise to Christ belong!
Hallelujah, Hallelujah,
Love and praise to Christ belong!

DIVINE *Healing*

CHAPTER 1

THE HOLY SPIRIT

THE HOLY SPIRIT

IT WAS A SATURDAY afternoon. The summer months were upon us, and therefore no school days. I was standing in line with other kids, waiting to go into the movie. I was 8 years old.

All of a sudden, while waiting for the ticket window to open, the Lord spoke to my heart. Now, I suspect that many would ask how I could know at 8 years of age that this was the Lord. Of course, the answer to that question is very easy. With the Lord being the Lord and able to do all things, He is perfectly able to make Himself known to whomever, even to an 8-year-old child.

Beyond a shadow of a doubt, I knew it was the Lord. He said to me, "Do not go into this place. Give me your heart, for you are a chosen vessel to be used exclusively in My service."

I stood transfixed, not knowing what to say or do. Then the ticket window opened, and the lady began handing out tickets to all the kids who were in the line.

The Lord spoke to me again, in effect, saying the very same thing: "Do not go into this place. Give me your heart, for you are a chosen vessel to be used exclusively in My service."

About that time, I approached the ticket window. I laid my quarter down, and then something happened that I know was the Lord. The ticket spool jammed, and while Mrs. Green was trying to untangle the problem, I grabbed my quarter and left. It was the greatest thing I ever did.

I walked past the Piggly Wiggly market, past Doris' Dress Shop, past the five-and-dime store, and then went into Vogt's Drugstore on the corner. I got myself an ice cream cone, walked out, and stood on the curb. All of a sudden it happened.

I've often wondered how individuals feel when they give their hearts to Christ, when they have been saved out of terrible sin. Of course, being only a child, I didn't know much about sin at all, but all of a sudden, the Spirit of God covered me. It was like 50 pounds were lifted from my frail shoulders, and I knew beyond a shadow of a doubt that I was saved. I never really said anything, except in my heart.

I arrived home very shortly thereafter, and my mother, knowing that I was in early, asked me what had happened.

I simply stated, "I got saved!" She looked somewhat nonplussed, but at the same time, she began to cry, and I knew she understood what I had said.

THE HOLY SPIRIT

A few days later, something happened that would further change my life for the better. I awakened early that morning and got up instantly and went into the living room. My mother and dad were standing beside my piano, and they were talking with each other. They were discussing my grandmother (my dad's mother). What they were saying was somewhat negative, but it did not strike me in that fashion. I listened intently.

My dad said, "Mama has gone crazy over religion." He then added, "Since she has come back from that meeting she attended, all she talks about is Jesus, and then she talks funny in a language that nobody can understand."

Now, my parents and my grandmother and grandfather all attended the same church. However, my grandmother was the very first one in our family to be baptized with the Holy Spirit with the evidence of speaking with other tongues.

I listened intently to what my dad said, and then, a few moments later, I bolted out of the room, got on my bicycle, and rode up to my grandmother's house. I wanted to know what she had.

As she let me in that morning (it was quite early), I said to her, "Nannie," for that's what I called her, "Mama and Daddy say that you speak in some kind of language that they can't understand. What are they talking about?"

I'll never forget it. Nannie laughed and said, "Come on in Jimmy, and I'll tell you all about it."

She was in the process of preparing some hot tea, and then she sat down in a chair with the hot tea on a little table beside the chair. I sat down on the floor with my legs crossed looking up at her. I wondered what she was going to say.

She began to tell me how that she had been baptized with the Holy Spirit with the evidence of speaking with other tongues. When she got to the part where the Lord filled her, the power of God came on her, and she raised both hands and began to speak with other tongues. Even though I had felt the convicting power of the Holy Spirit when I was saved that Saturday a short time before, I had really never felt the power of God, at least that I could remember.

But I felt it that morning! I looked down at my arms, and chill bumps had broken out all over. It was an experience that was to start me on a journey that continues unto this very hour so many, many years later.

I don't remember what transpired the rest of that meeting, but I came back that afternoon and asked her to tell it to me again, which she did. The same thing happened again. In fact, I went to her house from one to three times every day and had her tell me the same experience over and over until I knew it by heart. The reason for that was the power of God that would fall every time, and it would fall on me. Of course, I became very hungry to have what she had, and she encouraged me totally and completely, telling me that I could receive as well.

Incidentally, my mother and dad soon changed their attitude and allowed the Holy Spirit to work within their lives until they were both filled. However, let me tell you about the morning that the Lord filled me.

THE INFILLING OF THE HOLY SPIRIT

As stated, I was 8 years of age. We had started a prayer meeting in our little church, which I attended every morning.

This particular morning, as I began to ask the Lord to fill me, something happened that was beautiful.

I don't suppose there is such a thing as liquid light, but that's what seemed to rest upon me that morning. It formed a circle all around me. It could be seen with the actual eye, at least I could see it. Then I began to speak with other tongues as the Spirit of God gave the utterance, exactly as my grandmother had received.

It was a couple of weeks before I could speak English as I should. I would open my mouth and instantly begin to speak with other tongues. It didn't happen every time, but most of the time.

One particular morning, my mother sent me to the post office to get a stamp. I walked up to the window, laid the nickel on the counter, and opened my mouth to tell the man what I wanted, and I began to speak with other tongues.

He looked at me and said, "What did you say?" I didn't look like a foreigner, but I sounded like one. I tried it again and began to speak with other tongues.

He finally said, "Son, I can't understand what you're saying." I tried it again, and the same thing happened. It scared me, so I grabbed my nickel and ran.

When I got back home, my mother asked me if I had the stamp. I didn't, but then I could speak English. I explained to her what had happened.

I don't recall her response, but I do know that from then on, I was in a prayer meeting almost every day of my life, which went on for several years.

THE TALENT TO PLAY THE PIANO

Not long after I was baptized with the Holy Spirit, our little church was in a revival. The particular night in question, I was seated next to my dad. While the preacher was preaching, I began to ask the Lord to give me the talent to play the piano. I promised Him that I would never use it in the world but always for His glory.

When the service ended, with beautiful childlike faith, I walked up on the platform where the old upright piano was standing and began to make chords. I didn't know what they were, but I knew they sounded right.

When I got home that night, my Dad asked me, "Jimmy, where did you learn those chords on the piano? Have you been practicing at Aunt Stella's?"

Then he said, "Did the pastor's wife show you those chords?" The pastor's wife played piano quite well.

I said, "No, I haven't been practicing at all. I was asking the Lord tonight to give me the talent to play the piano, and I guess that He has already started."

To be sure, the Lord did exactly what I asked Him to do, and by His grace, I have kept that promise I made to Him to never use the talent in the world.

At 8 years of age, I knew I would be an evangelist. I knew my ministry would be worldwide. At that particular time, I did not know how all of that would come to pass, but I knew it would happen, and so it did. That is my calling—world evangelism.

THE DREAM

I must have been about 10 years of age when the Lord allowed me to see in a dream what the future would hold, at least some of the problems that would arise.

In the dream I was standing outside in front of our house where I was raised. As stated, I was about 10 years old.

I looked to my right, and there was a sphere hanging in space about 10 to 15 feet away from me. It was about the size of a basketball, and it was a globe of planet Earth. In the dream I could see it slowly turning.

Then, all of a sudden, I saw a figure standing right near that globe, looking intently at it as it slowly turned. Somehow, I knew it was Satan, and yet, there was no fear—none at all.

He looked at that globe intently for a short period of time and then turned, looked at me, and said, "You will not do it; I will stop you." I said nothing as he turned back to look at the globe. Then, once again, he turned and looked at me and said the same thing all over again: "You will not do it; I will stop you."

At that time I didn't know exactly that of which he was speaking. However, I came to understand in later years as I felt the full brunt of his efforts to stop us from carrying out that which God had called us to do.

THE HEALING

The following happened at about the time I was 10 years old as well.

The doctors did not know what was wrong with me. My parents took me to the physicians available in our little town, but they could find nothing wrong. They checked me for malaria and other things, but it was all to no avail.

I stayed nauseous constantly, and I would just simply pass out at times. It happened several times while I was at school, and my dad had to pick me up.

The last time this happened, my mother and dad went to get me, and the school principal told them, "If something is not done for Jimmy, you are going to have to take him out of school. We don't want him dying on our hands."

Of course, when I would go unconscious, it most definitely did cause consternation among the teachers, but, seemingly, there was nothing that could be done.

WHY?

During this time, I was anointed with oil and prayed for any number of times, but all to no avail.

It was a Sunday and the service had just ended. My mother and dad were going to take the pastor and his wife out to lunch, but they first had to go by the home of a parishioner and pray for the man who was ill.

I remember going into the back room with the others, praying for the brother, and then coming out to the front room to leave. My parents and others were making small talk, and then my dad said to the pastor, "Brother Culbreth, would you anoint Jimmy with oil and let's pray for him again?

If something isn't done, we're going to have to take him out of school."

I can still see it in my mind's eye. The pastor had a smile on his face and the little bottle of oil in his hands that he had just used to pray for the brother in question. He walked toward me and touched my forehead with the oil. Then it happened.

A BALL OF FIRE

It was like a ball of fire about the size of a softball that started at the top of my head and slowly went down my back. While it burned like fire, there was absolutely no pain whatsoever. It went down through my legs and out my feet, and I knew beyond the shadow of a doubt that I was healed. There was no doubt about it, I would never be sick with that problem again.

I have traveled all over the world, and I've eaten things at times that I think a dog wouldn't eat. Yet in all of those travels, spanning a time frame of several years, I got sick only one time, and then only for just an hour or so. In fact, I have had amazing health from then until now, and I attribute it all to that Sunday afternoon when the Lord healed me.

Does the Lord heal everyone in the same way, and I'm speaking of the ball of fire? No, He doesn't. I have met a few people through the years who were healed in the same manner; however, I've been prayed for regarding other situations, and I've never had that experience again. But I had it on that Sunday! It changed my world and changed my life. Jesus Christ still heals the sick.

I don't know why the Lord didn't heal me the preceding months. The same pastor, using the same bottle of oil, had anointed me several times, all to no avail. In fact, our entire church had prayed for me time and time again but to no avail. Why did the Lord wait till that particular Sunday afternoon? Was it something about the couple there that instigated the healing? No, it wasn't! I have no answer to these questions. I don't know why the Lord does all the things the way that He does, but there is one thing for which I thank Him—my mother and dad did not quit believing. They kept asking the Lord to heal my body, and that He did.

Looking back, I believe that Satan, knowing God would use me to see literally hundreds of thousands brought to a saving knowledge of Jesus Christ, tried to kill me. I believe that's exactly what happened, but, of course, the Lord did not permit such to come about.

THE BLINDED EYE NO LONGER BLIND

Frances and I were conducting a meeting at Brightmoor Tabernacle in Detroit, Michigan. This great church was built and pastored by Bond Bowman, one of the godliest men I ever knew. I preached two or three meetings in this great church, with each lasting for several weeks in duration.

If I remember correctly, it was a Friday night in the dead of winter, and snow was on the ground.

A young girl walked up to me, whom I did not know. I later learned that she was about 17 years old, very poor, and really didn't have suitable clothing for the type of weather that we were experiencing. I found out that she had hitchhiked every night to church, as dangerous as that was, but she wanted to be in those services so much that she would undertake the risk in order to be there.

The service ended that Friday night, and she walked up to me and said, "Brother Swaggart, can Jesus open a blinded eye?"

I looked at her and said, "Well, yes, He can. Why do you ask?"

She said to me, "My right eye is blind. Would you pray for me?"

(I actually cannot remember if it was her right or her left eye, but it was one.)

I laid hands on her and prayed for her as I had with others, and she turned and walked away.

A few moments later, I heard the associate pastor shouting, "Brother Swaggart! There has been a miracle!"

He pointed to the young lady, and I asked her to come to where I was on the platform, which she did.

I asked her to cover up her good eye, and then held up one finger, then two, while asking her how many fingers I was holding up. Each time, she gave me the correct answer.

THE MIRACLE THAT LASTS

Many years passed, and we were back in Detroit once again, this time in the coliseum, which seated thousands of people. It had been a great service that night. Actually, we were

only there for one night. The place was nearly full with thousands of people, and when the service was over, the moment
I stepped off the platform, I was seemingly surrounded by
hundreds of people.

I remember one man who stood about 6 feet 6 inches tall.
He picked me up like I was a rag doll and told me, "Brother
Swaggart, I was a member of the Black Panthers for years."
He went on to say, "I staggered home drunk on a Saturday
night, flipped on the television set, and drifted off into a
drunken sleep."

He then related to me how he awakened the next morning,
and the TV was still on. Actually, our program was on. He
lurched from the little cot to turn the TV to another channel,
but something stopped him. He leaned back and watched the
entirety of the service. When it ended, he was no longer a Black
Panther; he was saved by the precious blood of Jesus Christ.
He gave me his testimony that night.

As I was trying to get out the door, I was surrounded by
scores of people, with all of them acting so very gracious and
kind. Then this young lady pushed her way through to me.
She said, "Brother Swaggart, I don't think you recognize me,
do you?"

I looked at her, slowly shook my head and said, "No, I'm
sorry, but I don't think I do."

She then pointed to her eye and said, "It's still perfect from
the night that the Lord healed me." All of a sudden, it came
back. The tears rushed to my eyes as she stood there smiling
at me. She said, "I'm still healed."

Hallelujah what a thought,
Jesus full salvation brought,
Victory, yes victory.
Let the powers of sin assail,
Heaven's grace will never fail,
Victory, victory.

Victory, yes victory.
Hallelujah! I am free,
Jesus gives me victory,
Glory, glory, hallelujah!
He is all in all to me.

DIVINE *Healing*

CHAPTER 2

JESUS

JESUS

"AND WHEN JESUS WAS passed over again by ship unto the other side, much people gathered unto Him: and He was nigh unto the sea" (Mk. 5:21).

This means that hundreds, if not thousands of people were waiting on the shore for Him to come back to Capernaum.

AND WHEN JESUS WAS PASSED OVER AGAIN BY SHIP UNTO THE OTHER SIDE

The heading refers to Christ going back to Capernaum on the west side of the Sea of Galilee. In fact, even though He had been raised in Nazareth, His headquarters were now in Capernaum, located on the northwest corner of the lake, one might say. That which the Holy Spirit chose to serve as the headquarters of the Son of God during His earthly ministry was a beautiful setting. Actually, the entire north end and western side of the Sea of Galilee were ringed with towns, so we are told by Josephus, the Jewish historian.

MUCH PEOPLE GATHERED UNTO HIM

This speaks of a great crowd. Luke said, *"For they were all waiting for Him"* (Lk. 8:40). There were many who needed healing and who had perhaps come from afar. In fact, at least in the first year and a half of His ministry, anywhere that Jesus went, the crowds were thick and fast, with all types of problems being addressed—healings, demons cast out, etc. In fact, the name of Jesus was on the lips of every individual in Israel. Neither Israel nor anyone else for that matter had ever seen anything like Him. He never failed to heal. Whatever the problem was, no matter how severe it was, He healed them all. He never met a case that He could not change, a sick body He could not heal, or a demon possessed soul to whom He could not bring deliverance. As stated, there had never been anyone like Him and, in fact, there will never be anyone like Him again.

AND HE WAS NEAR UNTO THE SEA

Jesus departed out of the ship and was on the shore. He was met by hundreds, if not thousands, of people. The Sea of Galilee is about 14 miles long and about seven miles wide. As previously stated, it is the area that the Holy Spirit determined would be the headquarters of the Master. Today there are only a few ruins left. In fact, there's only one city on the Sea of Galilee at present—Tiberias.

If it is to be remembered, Jesus placed a curse upon the towns around the Sea of Galilee, with the exception of Tiberias.

In fact, there's no record that He ever went to Tiberias, and that is because it was mostly a Gentile enclave. As well, it is said that it was built over a graveyard, which would have defiled the Jews if they walked in that particular area. As it regards the towns around Galilee, especially on the northern and western shores, the Scripture says in the words of Christ, *"Woe unto you, Chorazin! woe unto you, Bethsaida! for if the mighty works had been done in Tyre and Sidon, which have been done in you, they had a great while ago repented, sitting in sackcloth and ashes"* (Lk. 10:13).

He then said, *"And thou, Capernaum, which are exalted unto heaven, shalt be brought down to hell: for if the mighty works, which had been done in you, had been done in Sodom, it would have remained until this day.*

"But I say unto you, That it shall be more tolerable for the land of Sodom, in the day of judgment, than for you" (Mat. 11:23-24).

"And, behold, there cometh one of the rulers of the synagogue, Jairus by name; and when he saw Him, he fell at His feet" (Mk. 5:22).

AND, BEHOLD, THERE COMETH ONE OF THE RULERS OF THE SYNAGOGUE

The words, *"And, behold,"* exclaim a happening of great significance that was about to take place. There were several rulers in each synagogue, of which Jairus was one. Their duties were to select the readers or teachers on the Sabbath, to examine their discourses, and to see that all things were done with decency and in accordance with ancestral usage.

JAIRUS BY NAME

The name Jairus meant "whom Jehovah enlightens." To be sure, he was to be enlightened more so than he could ever begin to realize.

Obviously, this was a man of some note, or else the Holy Spirit would not have devoted the time and attention to the situation as He did.

AND WHEN HE SAW HIM, HE FELL AT HIS FEET

The heading means that Jairus had heard that Jesus had arrived, and he rushed to seek His help. His request was preceded by His falling at Jesus' feet in a posture of worship because the need was so great, i.e., the saving of his daughter from death.

"And besought Him greatly, saying, My little daughter lies at the point of death: I pray You, come and lay Your hands on her, that she may be healed; and she shall live" (Mk. 5:23).

AND BESOUGHT HIM GREATLY

The heading proclaims an impassioned plea. One can well understand; his little daughter was dying! In fact, she would die before Jairus would be able to have Jesus come back with him; however, as we shall see, this would prove to be no hindrance to our Lord.

SAYING, MY LITTLE DAUGHTER LIES
AT THE POINT OF DEATH

As is obvious, the heading refers to the fact that the child was about to die. Actually, in a few minutes, someone would come from the home of Jairus and tell him that his daughter, in fact, was dead. In other words, she probably died about the time that her father was imploring Christ to come and heal her.

I PRAY YOU, COME AND LAY YOUR HANDS ON HER, THAT SHE MAY BE HEALED; AND SHE SHALL LIVE

The heading proclaims the fact that the man had faith in Jesus. Without a doubt, he had seen the Lord heal many in the preceding days; however, what he was about to see now would far eclipse what he had previously seen.

A point that should be brought out is the fact that the Gentile centurion had said to Jesus, *"Speak the word only,"* when referring to his servant, but the faith of Jairus does not seem to have risen to such degree (Mat. 8:5-13).

Divine healing refers to the fact that the Lord performs the work. As it regards that, I think these great experiences of Christ that are given to us in the Word will build faith in the heart and life of the believer as nothing else. Jesus Christ is the only divine healer. Men do not fall into that category, no matter how consecrated they are.

So, in giving these great illustrations, hopefully, it will build faith in your heart, and you will most of all understand that the one doing the healing is the Lord Jesus Christ. It was true then, and it is true now.

"And Jesus went with him; and much people followed Him, and thronged Him" (Mk. 5:24).

AND JESUS WENT WITH HIM

The heading proclaims a like response to the man's faith. If Jairus had requested Christ to speak the word as the centurion did, Jesus would have undoubtedly done so, and the child would have been healed or even raised from the dead at that moment. Nevertheless, Jesus met him on his own level and proceeded to go to his house.

This tremendous lesson of faith relative to comparing the centurion with Jairus must not be lost upon the reader. God responds to faith—at whatever level. However, He seldom seeks to increase faith at the moment, but rather responds to its present level, whatever that level may be. The level of faith receives the same level of response. Actually, Jesus at times would say, *"According to your faith be it unto you"* (Mat. 9:29).

Jesus also used terms such as, *"O you of little faith, wherefore did you doubt?"* (Mat. 14:31). In addition, He said, *"O woman, great is your faith"* (Mat. 15:28). So, we are made to see in these responses by Christ that there are levels of faith that receive the same level of response. Jairus seemed to need Jesus to come personally to his house, and even to physically lay His hands on his daughter. Consequently, that is what Jesus would do.

AND MUCH PEOPLE FOLLOWED
HIM, AND THRONGED HIM

The heading sets the stage for the next great miracle and another lesson in faith, which is astounding to say the least. The crowd was so intense around Christ that it almost suffocated Him. There were many people with many needs, and they knew that He alone had the answer. It hasn't changed from then until now. The only way that help can be received (I speak of help that will change the situation for the good) is from the Lord Jesus Christ. He is the source of all blessings and all things that we receive from God, while the Cross of Christ is the means.

In other words, it is the Cross that opened the door for Christ to be able to do all of these wonderful things. One might say that all the things that were done by the Lord before the Cross were done on credit, knowing that the Cross would ultimately pay the price, which it did.

What do we mean by the Cross being the means by which the Lord does all things?

First of all, when we speak of the Cross, we aren't speaking of the wooden beam on which Jesus died. We are rather speaking of what He there accomplished. What did He accomplish that made all of these things possible?

First of all, He atoned for all sin—past, present, and future—at least for all who will believe.

Paul wrote, *"By the which will we are sanctified through the offering of the body of Jesus Christ once for all"* (Heb. 10:10).

He then said, *"For by one offering He has perfected forever them who are sanctified"* (Heb. 10:14).

And then, *"This is the covenant that I will make with them after those days, says the Lord, I will put My laws into their hearts, and in their minds will I write them; and their sins and iniquities will I remember no more"* (Heb. 10:16-17).

At the Cross, Christ totally defeated Satan and all other fallen angels and demon spirits (Col. 2:10-15). How did He do that?

Sin gives Satan the legal right to do all that he does in that he steals, kills, and destroys, but with all sin atoned, Satan is defeated. He cannot hold anyone in bondage any longer, at least if one's trust is in Christ and what Christ did at the Cross.

The reader must understand that Jesus did not go to the Cross to appease Satan; He went to the Cross to appease God the Father. It was God to whom the price was owed. It was against God that man had sinned, and, therefore, the Cross was to right that wrong, pay that debt, and make things right with God the Father, which was done. So, when we say that the Cross of Christ is the means by which all of these wonderful things are given to us, that is the reason.

WHAT EXACTLY DID THE SACRIFICE OF CHRIST ADDRESS?

The sacrifice of Christ addressed everything that man lost in the fall, and I mean everything. Nothing was left unaddressed, unattended, or untouched. That means that all sin was atoned, all victory was won, and the door was opened for all things to be given to those who believe, and I mean all things. When Jesus said, *"It is finished,"* He meant that it was a finished work in totality. Let us say it again: Nothing was left undone. Jesus paid it all. That means that because of the Cross, if you will only believe, you can experience all spiritual blessings, all physical blessings, all material blessings, all financial blessings, and all domestic blessings (Rom. 6:3-14; I Cor. 1:17-18, 23; 2:2; Gal. 6:14; Col. 2:10-15). The Cross of Christ has made it all possible, and that we must ever understand and must never forget.

"And a certain woman, which had an issue of blood twelve years" (Mk. 5:25).

AND A CERTAIN WOMAN

This woman is said by tradition to have been named Veronica, a native of Caesarea Philippi.

There is, no doubt, any number of reasons the Holy Spirit included this dear lady (or anyone for that matter), considering that Jesus healed thousands, if not more. More than likely, she was included because of the uniqueness of the situation. As we shall see, this woman evidenced great faith in the face of difficult circumstances. To be sure, her faith was well rewarded.

WHICH HAD AN ISSUE OF BLOOD TWELVE YEARS

The heading speaks of a constant hemorrhage that she had suffered for 12 years, but she was now worse than ever as it regarded her physical condition. To be frank, I don't think it would be a stretch to say that the woman was dying. While she was still able to be mobile to a certain extent, common sense will tell you that she could not go on much longer in this particular state. However, her world was about to change.

"And had suffered many things of many physicians, and had spent all that she had, and was nothing bettered, but rather grew worse" (Mk. 5:26).

AND HAD SUFFERED MANY THINGS OF MANY PHYSICIANS

It actually means that she had suffered extreme pain at the hands of these so-called doctors, but to no avail. Luke, himself a physician, added, *"Which had spent all her living upon physicians, neither could be healed of any"* (Lk. 8:43). For sicknesses such as this, their manner of treatment in those days was primitive to say the least. In effect, there was really nothing they could do. As is here obvious, whatever they did, it mostly exacerbated the problem instead of relieving it.

AND HAD SPENT ALL THAT SHE HAD

The insinuation is that these doctors had attempted to treat her merely for the money they could receive out of it, knowing they could not help her. The implication is that she had once been quite wealthy but had spent basically all her worth on this effort to obtain relief.

Medicine in those days was most definitely not a science. There was more superstition involved in it than anything else, with very few people actually being helped. While the doctors of that time could help in minor cases, such as a boil, rash, etc., for something that was quite serious, there was nothing they could do.

**AND WAS NOTHING BETTERED,
BUT RATHER GREW WORSE**

The statement actually goes back to the previous phrase, lending credence to the thought that the physicians had not helped her at all but, if anything, had made the situation worse.

As we have previously stated, some of them treated her only for the money, knowing they could not help her.

So, I think as is obvious, this dear lady was in a perilous situation, but her world was about to change. How many millions down through the centuries have been in the same situation, whether physically or spiritually, or however or whatever, but they met Jesus. To be sure, they would never be the same again, with their lives given back to them. What a mighty God we serve!

"When she had heard of Jesus, came in the press behind, and touched His garment" (Mk. 5:27).

WHEN SHE HAD HEARD OF JESUS

This phrase has elicited more discussion than probably anything else said at this time.

Did it mean that she had never heard of Jesus before this particular time? That seems to be highly unlikely.

Jesus was constantly on the lips of every single individual in Israel. As we have previously stated, there had never been anyone like Him. He was healing every type of sickness, never failing even one time, no matter how hard the case was. So, to say that she had never heard of Jesus seems far-fetched.

Quite possibly she had made the trip to Capernaum for other reasons, and when she got there, somebody said that Jesus was soon to be there. The Greek actually says, "When she had heard of the Jesus," meaning that He had become so popular that even though this name was commonly used, still, He was distinguished from all others, hence, "the Jesus." (Jesus in the Hebrew means Joshua, which He was actually called.) It was quite a common name for the time and the place.

CAME IN THE PRESS BEHIND

The heading means that the moment Jesus disengaged from the ship and came ashore, hundreds of people surrounded Him, with many of them sick, some demon possessed, etc. So, when she arrived where He was, the scene was almost one of pandemonium. People were pulling and shoving, trying to get close to Him, and trying to touch Him. No doubt, she wondered in her weakened and sick condition how she could even get close to Him.

So, she somehow made her way through the crowd, which was at the back of our Lord.

AND TOUCHED HIS GARMENT

The heading probably referred to touching the hem of the shawl thrown over His shoulder. Even though there are indications that she may have been a Gentile, even with tradition saying so, this particular phrase seems to indicate that she may have been Jewish, although living in a Gentile area. Otherwise, it seems that she would have little knowledge or understanding respecting the touching of this part of His garment.

Concerning this hem or fringe, the Scripture says:

> *And the Lord spoke unto Moses, saying, Speak unto the children of Israel, and bid them that they make them fringes in the borders of their garments throughout their generations, and that they put upon the fringe of the borders a ribband (ribbon) of blue: And it shall be unto you for a fringe, that you may look upon it, and remember all the commandments of the Lord, and do them; and that you seek not after your own heart and your own eyes, after which you use to go a whoring* (Num. 15:37-39).

This commandment concerning the fringe of the garment was to make it visible to all of Israel that they were a heavenly people, and that this great fact should especially be present to their hearts when necessarily coming in closest touch with the earth. It was to be worn on the outer garment and on each of the four corners as a tassel of blue:

Pulpit said, "The tasseled Hebrew was a marked man in other eyes and in his own; he could not pass himself off as one of the heathen. He was perpetually reminded of the special relation in which he stood to the Lord."

In other words, he wore the colors of the Lord. That color was blue, reminding him that his help came from above.

"For she said, If I may touch but His clothes, I shall be whole" (Mk. 5:28).

FOR SHE SAID

The heading means that she kept saying over and over to herself, or even possibly to others nearby, *"If I may touch but His clothes, I shall be whole."*

So, as stated, this tells me that she was Jewish inasmuch as she understood what was meant by the shawl with the ribbon of blue that was thrown over His shoulder, which every Jewish man wore.

In all of this, we must come to the conclusion that something had transpired within her heart respecting a way to be healed. No doubt, she would have loved to approach Him with the opportunity to tell Him of her difficulties and problems. However, as is now obvious, such was not possible. The crowd was too great, with too many clamoring to get to Him.

So, the Holy Spirit dropped a word within her heart that generated faith and found a way, as faith will always find a way. She would touch the hem of His garment (Lk. 8:44).

IF I MAY TOUCH BUT HIS CLOTHES,
I SHALL BE WHOLE

Jairus wanted Jesus to touch his daughter, while this *"certain woman"* knew that with her, this was not possible; therefore, she would touch Him instead of Him touching her. The entire scenario tells us, as stated, that faith will find a way. It will not take no for an answer, and neither will it be hindered by seemingly impossible circumstances.

So, if Jesus has not touched you, that doesn't mean that all hope is gone. You can touch Him! If you touch Him by faith and with faith, you will receive just as much as if He had touched you. This dear woman proves that truth. This opens up the possibility for the receiving of whatever is needed to any and all. No one is excluded except those who will not believe.

THE POWER OF GOD

Sometimes the power of God is so real that the Lord touches all in the place, or at least some, but sometimes there is no touch. But yet, according to this woman, whatever is needed can still be obtained. I believe that this is at least a part of the lesson the Holy Spirit desires that we learn. Even though He may not touch you, you can touch Him!

What does it mean to touch the Lord?

Well, regarding this *"certain woman,"* who was, no doubt, inspired by the Holy Spirit, she realized that she would not be able to get Him to touch her, so she reasoned in her mind and spirit that she could touch Him and the effect would be the same. It was! It was just that simple.

However, because Jesus is not here physically as then, the situation presently is a tiny bit different. The difference is that it only requires a slightly higher level of faith. In effect, He is here, just not physically. When individuals are in a church service, or wherever, and the Spirit and power of God are moving greatly, with many being touched and healed, it doesn't really take nearly the faith as this of which we speak. However, at these times, some, if not many, do not receive a touch from the Lord. They are then led to believe (because of the lack of obvious evidence) that they are not able to receive what others have received. This passage tells us differently.

I can see far down the mountain,
Where I have wandered weary years,
Often hindered on my journey
By the ghosts of doubts and fears;
Broken vows and disappointments
Thickly strewn along the way,
But the Spirit (the Divine Spirit) led unerring,
To the land I hold today.

DIVINE *Healing*

CHAPTER 3

NO FORMULA

NO FORMULA

THERE IS NO FORMULA given in the Word of God concerning receiving from the Lord. The reason is obvious: All individuals and their situations are unique. Faith always requires different things of different people. Consequently, the formulas given by most preachers simply do not work. Therefore, one must understand that no formula is available. The few steps I will give also must not be construed as a formula.

THE WILL OF GOD

As with the woman with the issue of blood, individuals must settle it in their minds that it is the will of God for them to receive from the Lord. If they vacillate on this point, it shows a lack of faith. We must believe that *"He* (God) *is, and that He is a rewarder of them who diligently seek Him"* (Heb. 11:6).

James told us that faith cannot work in a double-minded atmosphere. He said, *"A double minded man is unstable in all his ways"* (James 1:8). He also said, *"But let him ask in faith, nothing wavering"* (James 1:6).

GOD'S WORD

As the woman with the issue of blood, touching the Lord must be anchored in God's Word, in other words, claiming His promises. In effect, this is exactly what she did. She must have had an inkling of knowledge as to what this blue tassel on Jesus' garment meant. Therefore, she touched it—and in faith! So, claim the Word for your particular case and believe it. Understand, as well, that what Jesus did for you at the Cross opens the door for great and wonderful things. In fact, the Cross of Christ gives us much greater access than what this dear lady had so long ago, or anyone else before the Cross for that matter.

PERSEVERE

Persevere until the answer comes. This is where many believers break down. They do the things mentioned, and no answer is forthcoming, at least at that particular time. They soon grow weary and quit. The Holy Spirit desires that we keep believing even though circumstances may say the opposite, as they often do. The answer will come even though at times it may be delayed. As stated, and by now should be obvious, it is not nearly as simple to touch the Lord as it is for Him to touch us. But it can be done, as evidenced by this dear lady.

This passage was given by the Holy Spirit for this very purpose. *"And straightway the fountain of her blood was dried up; and she felt in her body that she was healed of that plague"* (Mk. 5:29).

AND STRAIGHTWAY THE FOUNTAIN
OF HER BLOOD WAS DRIED UP

The heading contains a powerful meaning. It not only means that the bleeding instantly stopped, but that which caused the bleeding (the fountain, if you please) was instantly dried up. In other words, she was totally and completely healed. While she would ultimately grow old and die, it would not be from this disease.

AND SHE FELT IN HER BODY THAT SHE
WAS HEALED OF THAT PLAGUE

The heading means that she had felt oftentimes the efforts of the doctors attempting to help her but only hurting her. As she felt that, she felt this, but with a great difference. Then she felt pain; now she felt healing! Because of what she felt in her body, she knew beyond the shadow of a doubt that *"she was healed of that plague."* And so she was! The cure was instantaneous.

Let us say it once again that doctors of that time had absolutely no similarity whatsoever to the medical profession presently. Today medicine is a science and, therefore, is somewhat predictable. I thank God for modern medicine, for doctors, for nurses, for hospitals, etc. I thank the Lord for the knowledge that He has given individuals in these last days as it regards the medical profession. No, our taking medicine or being under the care of a doctor does not harm our faith or diminish it whatsoever. While, of course, the Lord doesn't need anything to heal anyone, still, as every believer knows, while the Lord does heal, He doesn't heal every time. Thank God, at times He helps us by using the medical knowledge of a doctor, or whatever the case. Sometimes it seems that He affords no help whatsoever from any source, but we are still to believe.

"And Jesus, immediately knowing in Himself that virtue had gone out of Him, turned Him about in the press, and said, Who touched My clothes?" (Mk. 5:30).

AND JESUS, IMMEDIATELY KNOWING IN HIMSELF THAT VIRTUE HAD GONE OUT OF HIM

The heading tells us a couple of things. First, that which was done by Christ for others had a price tag attached to it, as is obvious in this verse, at least as it pertains to Him. Virtue (power) went out of Him. This would have had some effect on Him physically, emotionally, and spiritually. Second, we learn from this the tremendous power of faith in God.

In mid-1995, Frances and I were in a series of evangelistic meetings in Mexico, with a couple of services on the United States side of the border. We were to be in Harlingen, Texas, on that particular Monday night. I was almost ready to leave for the service that night when I greatly sensed the presence of the Lord. My mind was on the message I would preach that evening, which was this very text.

The Lord spoke to my heart, saying: "I'm going to show you something about this illustration of the woman touching

the hem of My garment that you have not previously seen."
Actually, as my memory comes back, even as I dictate these
notes, some of it began to unfold even then; however, it was
only during the message that the Spirit of God greatly outlined
that which He had spoken.

The auditorium was jammed to capacity that night, and,
correspondingly, there was a mighty moving of the Holy Spirit
in the entirety of the service.

A MESSAGE OF FAITH

As I preached, I was greatly sensing the presence of the
Lord, with the congregation sensing it as well. I came to the
part regarding the woman touching the hem of Jesus' garment.
When I got to that part, the Holy Spirit fully brought out that
which He had given me in part before the service. It was as
follows: Jesus did not know this woman was in the crowd, did
not know of her illness, did not know of her determination to
receive her healing, and actually didn't even know she existed.
As stated, the Holy Spirit did not see fit to reveal this to Him,
perhaps for the very reason I'm about to give.

Her experience portrays to any and all that faith in God
is such a powerful force, even such a powerful commodity if
you please, that it would pull healing from Jesus even though
He did not even know this woman existed. As I began to
expound this to the congregation, you could sense faith building greatly in the audience. As well, it was so powerful on me
all night long that I actually slept very little. On the way to the

airport the next morning, it increased respecting that which the Lord had given me.

God loves faith! Actually, one cannot even please God without faith (Heb. 11:6). He wants His children to believe Him! If something was so powerful (as this obviously was) that it would bring healing from Christ even though He did not even know the woman existed, then we're talking about something that is powerful beyond our comprehension. All believers should diligently seek to increase their faith in the Lord and God's Word. In fact, such is done by the diligent study of the Word of God, for *"faith comes by hearing, and hearing by the Word of God"* (Rom. 10:17).

This is the reason that I have used these illustrations from the ministry of the Master to illustrate the great doctrine of divine healing.

TURNED HIM ABOUT IN THE PRESS AND, SAID, WHO TOUCHED MY CLOTHES?

In the Greek it actually says, "Who touched Me on My clothes?" As the next verse proclaims, there was a great press of people around Him, and many were attempting to touch Him, but without any recorded results. The difference was that this woman had faith. Consequently, He felt it.

"And His disciples said unto Him, You see the multitude thronging You, and You say, Who touched Me?" (Mk. 5:31).

The disciples were not privileged to know what was going on, but the Lord knew something had happened—something wonderful.

AND HIS DISCIPLES SAID UNTO HIM

They did not understand His question, especially considering that scores of people were pressing Him, even thronging Him, and consequently touching Him. What did He mean, *"Who touched My clothes?"*

Consequently, we see from this act of faith performed by this dear woman that the only thing she actually needed was faith in God. She didn't have to go through the disciples and, in fact, did not do so. So, that shoots down the Roman Catholic appeal to dead saints, or live ones for that matter. She went personally to Jesus without Him even knowing she was there. By her faith she was able to receive exactly what she needed.

YOU SEE THE MULTITUDE THRONGING
YOU, AND YOU SAY, WHO TOUCHED ME?

The heading portrays that this was completely beyond Peter's understanding, or any of the other disciples for that matter (Lk. 8:45).

Why would one touching Him mean more or be different than others touching Him?

The difference was faith!

Why did this woman have faith and the others did not?

There is no answer to that. Actually, they should have had more faith than she did. They had already witnessed many of the miracles of Christ, while she had only recently heard what Jesus could do, or so it seems. But yet, she had great faith in Christ.

From the time the Lord spoke to my heart in Harlingen, Texas, respecting this truth that I have attempted to relate to you, I have sensed an urgency of the Holy Spirit respecting the increase of my faith. It's as if He's telling me, "Do not look at circumstances or situations, but look to Me and believe Me." I have sensed and felt that as never before. As well, I believe it is faith that will be used to touch untold millions for the cause of Christ. God never does anything of this nature but that it is for an intended purpose.

LOOK WHAT THE LORD HAS WROUGHT!

From that time (1995), the Lord has done wondrous things for this ministry. In 1997, the Lord gave me the great Word of the Cross and, as well, how the Holy Spirit works within our lives. In the year 2000, He gave me the SonLife Radio Network, broadcasting the gospel 24 hours a day, seven days a week, now on some 74 radio stations. In 2005, He gave me The Expositor's Study Bible, which has sold more than 3 million copies.

In 2010, the Lord instructed me to begin the SonLife Broadcasting Television Network. As of this writing, we are going by television into 90 million homes in America, seven days a week, 24 hours a day. As well, we are going into nearly 300 million homes in cities outside the United States, plus the satellites and the Internet. In fact, I'm told that more than 2 billion people can tune in to the SonLife Broadcasting Network if they so desire. As I dictate these notes, I believe that the Lord has told me that a move of God is coming that will be the last great move before the coming great tribulation. It will usher hundreds of thousands, if not millions, into the kingdom of God.

We must never forget, *"Jesus Christ* (is) *the same yesterday, and today, and forever"* (Heb. 13:8).

THE LORD LOOKS FOR THOSE
WHO EXHIBIT FAITH IN HIM

"And He looked round about to see her who had done this thing" (Mk. 5:32). Irrespective of the question Peter had asked, Jesus began a scrutinizing gaze in search for the woman. It is amazing how the Holy Spirit works. Jesus knew someone had touched Him with great faith, but that is as much as the Spirit gave to Him.

He did not tell Him where the woman was in the crowd, and at this stage, I don't think Christ even really knew if it was a woman or a man. All of this was for purpose. There is a possibility that the woman was very shy. Then again, because of her disease, she had actually broken the law of Moses by touching Him. In other words, she was unclean. Consequently, the Holy Spirit would give her time to compose herself before she would give her testimony.

She had only touched the garment and had not by any means grabbed it. Therefore, His knowing of this touch was

not because of its action but because of what it represented—
her faith.

While it was unlawful for her to touch the Lord due to her
particular physical malady, still, this was only a ceremonial
law and by no means a moral law. Consequently, the law of
faith that she evidenced overrode this ceremonial law exactly
as it did when David ate the shewbread, thereby, breaking a
ceremonial law (I Sam. 21).

*"But the woman fearing and trembling, knowing what was
done in her, came and fell down before Him, and told Him all the
truth"* (Mk. 5:33).

This passage proclaims her now seeking mercy as she had
previously sought healing, and it would also be granted!

BUT THE WOMAN FEARING AND TREMBLING

The heading pictures something going on in her soul. Luke
prefaced this statement by saying, *"And when the woman saw
that she was not hid"* (Lk. 8:47).

Perhaps the consternation was caused by the knowledge
that inasmuch as she was unclean, she had broken a ceremonial law by touching Christ. She had not asked His permission, carrying out her act of faith, so to speak, behind the
scenes. Now He had stopped the entire procession and was
looking earnestly through the crowd and proclaiming that
virtue had gone out of Him. She was found out, but the results
wouldn't be what she had feared. This she did know: the disease was gone.

KNOWING WHAT WAS DONE IN HER

First of all, and as stated, the woman knew the disease was gone. Considering that she had spent all her living on doctors for some 12 years and had grown no better, but rather worse, there was no doubt in her mind or body that she was healed of that plague. Actually, she could feel it deep within her that the problem was gone. Furthermore, she would never be troubled with it again. It was a complete and permanent cure.

And yet, she was fearful that she had done something wrong. No doubt she knew of the strict censure of the Pharisees. Not knowing Jesus before now, due to living a goodly distance away (according to tradition), she wondered if He might be angry.

CAME AND FELL DOWN BEFORE HIM

As stated, the heading proclaims her seeking mercy as she had previously sought healing. This much she did know: Anyone who (as Jesus) had that type of power manifested was more than ordinary and deserved worship, which she freely gave! She did not know what He might do, but she did know what had already been done. She had been gloriously and wondrously healed, and of that there was no doubt.

Can you imagine how this dear lady felt, knowing that she was healed, especially after suffering for some 12 years? She would never be the same again, and no wonder! How many millions down through the centuries has the Lord changed their lives exactly as He did this dear lady? How many in the world today can say the same thing as that dear lady of so long ago?

AND TOLD HIM ALL THE TRUTH

These six words of the heading proclaim in beautiful simplicity that this woman shared exactly the thoughts of her heart concerning the touching of the hem of His garment. Luke, being a doctor, added the words, *"How she was healed immediately"* (Lk. 8:47).

Tell it to Jesus, Tell it to Jesus,
He is a friend that's well-known;
You've no other such a friend or brother,
Tell it to Jesus alone.

She told everything exactly as it had happened. In her heart of hearts she knew that anyone who had such power would also know if she told otherwise.

"And He said unto her, Daughter, your faith has made you whole; go in peace, and be whole of your plague" (Mk. 5:34).

In verse 25, she was addressed merely as a certain woman. Now she is called daughter, which signifies relationship. He, in effect, had made her a member of the family of God.

As someone has said:

- She was chained.
- She was changed.
- She was claimed.

AND HE SAID UNTO HER, DAUGHTER

First of all, the word *daughter* was a word of endearment. In effect, He was claiming her as a member of the family, so to speak. Not only was she healed, but she was now saved as well. She was now a member of the family of God.

It was the same family to which the disciples belonged, as well as all who have prostrated themselves as she did before the lowly Galilean. Even though she was near His age, or possibly even older, His use of the word *daughter* proclaimed Him as the Messiah; therefore, He spoke as a father to a daughter.

THE REMEDY ALONE IS CHRIST AND HIM CRUCIFIED

This entire episode has a far greater meaning than just the healing of an individual, as wonderful and gracious as that was. It is obvious here that this malady represents to us the ever-flowing bitter fountain of sin, for which no treatment can be found in human philosophy. The remedy is only to be found in Christ and what He did for us at the Cross.

Pulpit said, "To touch Christ's garment is to believe in His incarnation, whereby He has touched us and so has enabled us by faith to touch Him and to receive His salvation of grace."

As stated, there is no earthly remedy for sin, but there is a remedy. That remedy is Christ and Him crucified—and Christ and Him crucified alone!

YOUR FAITH HAS MADE YOU WHOLE

The heading carries a powerful statement. He said to her, *"Your faith,"* implying the ingredient that one must have in order to receive from God, be it physical, financial, domestic, or spiritual. The word *faith* is central to the Christian experience and message. And yet, at times this word is corrupted by a misunderstanding of its true biblical meaning.

Oftentimes, people use the word *faith* to indicate what is possible but uncertain. This is what causes most people to not receive from the Lord. The Bible uses the word *faith* in ways that link it with what is assuredly and certainly true. Consequently, this is the type of faith that this woman had and that all are demanded to have, that is, if we are to receive from the Lord. The object of our faith must not be ourselves or others, but rather Jesus Christ and Him crucified, and that alone (Rom. 6:3-14; I Cor. 1:17-18, 21, 23; 2:2; Gal. 6:14).

There is no limit to what faith in God can do. It holds out a promise to all of mankind that a personal relationship with God in Jesus Christ can literally transform any situation.

THE OBJECT OF FAITH MUST EVER BE
JESUS CHRIST AND HIM CRUCIFIED

The Old Testament speaks of false sources of security. It holds each of them up and examines them in contrast to the security that is ours in the Lord, and in the Lord alone. Over and over again it proclaims the foolishness of man in turning from reliance on God in order to seek the security of other men (Ps. 118:8; 146:3; Jer. 17:5).

We are also warned not to have faith in riches (Ps. 49:6; 52:7), military power (Deut. 28:52; Ps. 44:6; Jer. 5:17), or in our own goodness (Ezek. 33:13; Hos. 10:13). True faith fastens on God as one who, by His nature, is the sole certainty and sure reality. God is faithful and unchanging, established in eternity. Because He is who He is, we can commit ourselves to Him.

We have faith in God by understanding that His Son, our Saviour, the Lord Jesus Christ, is the source of all blessings, whatever those blessings might be. However, the means by which all of this comes to us is the Cross of Christ, and the Cross alone.

Let me say it this way:
- The only way to God the Father is through Jesus Christ (Jn. 14:6).
- The only way to Jesus Christ is by the Cross (Lk. 9:23).
- The only way to the Cross is a denial of self, i.e., denying our own strength, personal ability, etc. (Lk. 9:23).

As our faith is anchored in Christ and what He has done for us at the Cross, God the Father commits Himself to us in covenant relationship. The placing of our confidence in Him brings us true well-being and safety.

THE OLD TESTAMENT VIEW OF FAITH

In Old Testament times (which also carries over into the present), God demanded that those who followed Him do so because He is utterly faithful and trustworthy. In the great faith worthies, the New Testament points to Abraham as faith's primary example. Genesis, Chapter 15, describes Abraham, then a very old man, in dialogue with God. Abraham complained that God had given him no children of his own despite an earlier promise (Gen. 12:2). God responded by amplifying the promise. Abraham looked to the sky, filled with its numberless stars, and heard God say, *"So shall your seed be"* (Gen. 15:5).

The next verse tells us, *"And he* (Abraham) *believed in the* LORD; *and He counted it to him for righteousness"* (Gen. 15:6).

The apostle Paul says of this incident:

> *Who* (Abraham) *against hope believed in hope, that he might become the father of many nations; according to that which was spoken, So shall your seed be. And being not weak in faith, he considered not his own body now dead, when he was about an hundred years old, neither yet the deadness of Sarah's womb: He staggered not at the promise of God through unbelief; but was strong in faith, giving glory to God; and being fully persuaded that, what He* (the Lord) *had promised, He was able also to perform* (Rom. 4:18-21).

Abraham examined the circumstances and despite everything, decided that God was to be trusted. Abraham consciously chose to put his trust in God. This act of saving faith was accepted by the Lord in place of a righteousness that Abraham, within himself, did not possess. Abraham was not perfect by any standard, as the Scriptures bear out, but his life, as recorded in the Old Testament, shows again and again that he trusted God and acted on God's promises, certain that he could count on the Lord (Heb. 11:8-12).

THE EXAMPLE

The example of Abraham stands as the biblical illustration of faith as a believing response to God. God spoke in promise and command. Abraham trusted himself to God, and Abraham's faith was demonstrated as he subsequently acted on what God had said (Gen. 12-22).

Concerning Abraham's faith, Jesus said, *"Your father Abraham rejoiced to see My day: and he saw it, and was glad"* (Jn. 8:56). What did Jesus mean by Abraham seeing *"My day"*? He was speaking of the fact that everything that the Lord had shown Abraham, as it regarded justification by faith, depended totally upon the coming of the Redeemer, who was to come through the lineage of Isaac, the son of Abraham and Sarah. The Redeemer also would have to die in order to redeem fallen humanity. This great truth was given to Abraham as it regarded the command of the Lord for Abraham to offer up Isaac in sacrifice, which, as is known, was stopped at the last moment (Gen. 22).

However, even though the Lord showed Abraham that redemption would come by and through the death of the Redeemer (Gen. 22:13-14), He didn't show the Patriarch how that death would come about. That revelation was given to Moses, and we speak of the Cross. It concerned the serpent on the pole (Num. 21:4-9).

Jesus mentioned this, as well. He said, *"And as Moses lifted up the serpent in the wilderness, even so must the Son of Man be lifted up* (which spoke of the Cross): *That whosoever believes in Him should not perish, but have eternal life"* (Jn. 3:14-15).

So, it has always been the Cross (Gen. 3:15).

AN EXAMPLE OF UNBELIEF OR LACK OF FAITH

While a study of Abraham's life helps us to understand the nature of belief or faith, by contrast the history of the generation of Israelites who were redeemed from Egypt helps us to understand the nature of unbelief. Exodus 4:1-8 is the foundation, and Numbers 14 is the culmination of a theme.

Exodus 4 reports a dialogue between the Lord and a hesitant Moses. Moses had been told to return to Egypt. He would become the instrument of Israel's deliverance. However, Moses objected: *"But, behold, they will not believe me, nor hearken unto my voice: for they will say, The LORD has not appeared unto you"* (Ex. 4:1).

God gave Moses the power to perform three miracles and explained: *"And it shall come to pass, if they will not believe you, neither hearken to the voice of the first sign, that they will believe the voice of the latter sign"* (Ex. 4:8).

The book of Hebrews warns New Testament believers not to permit a hardened heart to drag them into error. If that happens, they will become like the evil generation that heard God's Word, but the unbelieving heart was shown by their refusal to obey (Heb. 3:12). The stories of Abraham and of the Exodus generation show the meaning of faith in positive and negative terms. Through them we see several basic aspects of faith.

THE BASICS OF FAITH

First, faith is not some response to evidence, even when that evidence is clearly miraculous. Abraham believed God. His faith was a response to God Himself, who met Abraham directly in a word of promise. That word from God is far more compelling for faith than any miracles performed in the material universe.

Second, faith in God engages the total person. It is expressed in presumption and action and by the word *believing*. In fact, believing is the action part of faith.

Abraham was well aware of his and Sarah's advanced age, but Abraham also considered God's power and faithfulness. The fact of God so transformed Abraham's perspective that he easily accepted God's promise, although fathering a son was humanly impossible for him. But Israel, poised on the borders of Canaan, could see only the military strength of that land's inhabitants. They treated God with contempt (Num. 14:11; 16:30) by refusing to consider His power and reality.

ACTION

Faith is also expressed in actions. When Abraham was told to go to Canaan, he packed up and went (Gen. 12). When the Exodus generation was told to conquer the land, they refused even to try. They were betrayed by their unbelieving hearts.

Third, the outcome of faith was demonstrated. When a person responds to God's self-disclosure, faith-generated obedience leads to blessing. Abraham believed God and knew God's protection during his lifetime. Conversely, the unbelieving generation of Israelites wandered back into the wilderness to die in its desolate wastes.

FAITH AS EXPRESSED IN THE NEW TESTAMENT

The object of faith in the New Testament (as in the Old) continues to be God, but now, it is through Jesus, who is a reality, whereas in the Old Testament, He was only a shadow. Consequently, faith, as expressed in the New Testament and in Christ, is far more developed than in the Old. The reason is clearly expressed by Jesus Himself: *"I am the way, the truth, and the life: no man comes unto the Father, but by Me"* (Jn. 14:6). God the Father has revealed Himself in the Son. The Father has set Jesus before us as the one to whom we must entrust ourselves for salvation. It is Jesus who must be the focus of Christian faith and, more particularly, what He did for us at the Cross (Eph. 2:13-18).

In the context of our faith and in our relationship with Jesus, which are inseparable, *believing* has come to mean:

- The happy trust that a person places in the person of Jesus and what He has done for us at the Cross.
- The allegiance to Him that grows out of that very personal commitment.

FAITH AS EXPRESSED IN THE GOSPELS

The Gospels report many signs (miracles) that Jesus performed as He traveled and taught. Often, but not always, Jesus' healings were intimately associated with the faith of the sick person, exactly as is expressed in this woman who touched the hem of His garment (Mat. 9:2, 22, 29; Mk. 2:5; 5:34; Lk. 17:19; 18:42).

However, a survey of the Gospels shows that for most of the people, Jesus' miracles failed to produce true faith. Even as Jesus hung on the Cross, the mocking promise of His watching enemies was alive. *"Now come down from the Cross,"* they pledged, *"and we will believe"* (Mat. 27:42; Mk. 15:32). Also, when Jesus was raised from the dead, what happened? These men were the first to attempt to hide the evidence (Mat. 28:11-15).

In this we see the phenomenon we note in the Old Testament report of ancient Israel's unbelief. The exodus miracles provided incontrovertible proof of God's power and His presence. Yet, the Exodus generation would not commit themselves to Him. The nation in Jesus' day saw His healings, watched Him cast out demons, and even saw Him raise Lazarus from the dead; yet they refused to believe.

BELIEVING

Belief in the full flow of God's power was difficult, even for the disciples. They had trusted themselves to Jesus as the Son of God, but when the Lord was crucified, their hope and confidence drained away. On the day of the resurrection, they could not bring themselves to believe that the One they trusted had come to life again (Mat. 28, Mk. 16, Lk. 24). However, in the Gospels, one vital fact is made clear in Jesus' words about faith: A lack of trust in God in whom we have faith closes off life's possibilities. When we fail to believe, we do not experience the full range of God's activity (Mat. 21:22), but when we trust, we open up our future to a full experience of God's power (Mat. 17:20; 21:21; Lk. 7:9-10). All things are possible to the one who believes.

For you and me, faith in Jesus does not come through an observation of miracles, as wonderful as they may be. Faith is born as we learn about Jesus, find out what He said and what He did for us as it refers to the Cross, and then put our trust in Him. We then go on to deeper faith and active reliance on the power and presence of God. As we trust, our life opens up to all sorts of possibilities. Miracles follow faith. Believing, we experience God at work in our lives.

FAITH AS LOOKED AT BY JOHN THE BELOVED

John looks at the relationship between believing and evidence. He examines superficial belief, and he connects true faith with life and death. In addition, several passages of John's gospel called for careful study. In Christian faith, knowing and believing are linked. We respond to testimony about Jesus with our intellects as well as with our hearts. John's gospel looks at two kinds of testimony: there is the testimony of Jesus' miracles and the testimony of Jesus' words.

At times these two lines of testimony enhance each other. Thus, the Twelve, who were already committed to Jesus, saw the miracle at Cana of Jesus turning the water into wine (Jn. 2:11) and found their belief in Jesus strengthened. It is not unusual to find that many of the observers of Jesus' works were moved to some kind of belief. The testimony of His miracles was compelling (Jn. 7:31; 11:45; 12:11). Yet, others who saw the same signs chose not to believe, rejecting Jesus against the evidence of the Lord's works (Jn. 10:38; 14:11).

In John we see that the testimony provided by miracles and signs forced observers to take Jesus seriously, but signs and miracles alone do not bring about saving faith.

SUPERFICIAL BELIEF

John distinguishes between two types of believing. His gospel was written, he told his readers, *"that you might believe that Jesus is the Christ, the Son of God; and that believing you might have life through His name"* (Jn. 20:31). Yet, when John describes the response of the crowds to the testimony of Jesus' miracles, it is clear that those who believed did so in a way that fell short of life-giving belief in Jesus as the Son of God.

John 2:22-23 tells us of many who saw His signs and believed in Him. But later, after that same crowd of shallow disciples heard Jesus speak about Himself as the Bread of Life (Jn., Chpt. 6), they complained: *"This is an hard saying; who can hear it?"* (Jn. 6:60). John observes that *"From that time many of His disciples went back, and walked no more with Him"* (Jn. 6:66).

Superficial faith came in response to the miraculous, and it died when Jesus communicated the divine content of His message. Nicodemus, a religious leader, confessed, *"We know that You are a teacher come from God: for no man can do these miracles that You do, except God be with Him"* (Jn. 3:2). Yet, when other religious leaders heard the message that Jesus spoke (Jn. 7:16-17), they refused to go on to the belief that involved commitment to Jesus as Lord (Jn. 7:45-47). Wonder at Jesus' powers, even agreement that God must have sent Him, falls short of saving faith.

Only when one recognizes Jesus as the Son of God and commits himself completely to Him does a person believe in the fullest saving sense. This commitment involves accepting His words and making them the framework of one's life.

FAITH AND LIFE

Over and over in his writings, John links faith with life and unbelief with death. The one who believes in Jesus has eternal life. The one who does not believe is already condemned to eternal death. The intimate connection between life and believing is as marked in John's gospel and epistles as is the connection between faith and righteousness in the writings of Paul.

Chapter 8 of John's gospel explores the link between the testimony of the miraculous and the testimony of the message. Jesus teaches clearly that He and the Father are inseparably one. Thus, belief in Jesus is the critical issue for every hearer: *"For if you believe not that I am He, you shall die in your sins"* (Jn. 8:24).

The miracles of Jesus, likewise, cannot be argued away, but when Jesus spoke the truth, the religious leaders attacked Him. Unlike Abraham, who heard God speak and responded with belief in the Lord, this generation did not respond to the Word of Truth. When the physical descendants of Abraham rejected the fresh word of God that came through Jesus, they proved themselves to be of a different spiritual family, for Abraham believed God, but these men refused to believe God's Son.

THE MIRACLE OF LAZARUS

Chapter 11 of John's gospel tells the story of the raising of Lazarus from the dead. While many accepted the testimony of the miracle and accepted Jesus' word about Himself, the story itself looks at believing from a slightly different perspective. Mary and Martha, the sisters of Lazarus, did believe in Jesus. They believed that Jesus, as the source of life, would raise Lazarus *"at the last day"* (Jn. 11:24), for Jesus was the Christ and the Son of God (Jn. 11:27). However, although saving faith was present, the women still failed to understand the life-giving power of Jesus, power that enabled Him to raise their brother then and there, recalling him to life, even though he had been dead for four days.

This proclaims to us that one may have saving faith in Jesus, as the sisters of Lazarus, and yet, limit His power. When we put our trust in Jesus, the Son of God, we enter a relationship with one who is Lord, and whose ability to act in our world is without limitations. Actually, this characterizes the greater majority of the modern church. Saving faith in Christ is believed and maintained, yet, many limit Him thereafter!

PAUL AND FAITH

To Paul fell not only the task of presenting the gospel but also of giving testimony and explanation. Consequently, he dealt with faith and salvation, faith and righteousness, and faith and fellowship with God. In the first three chapters of Romans, Paul demonstrated the fact that all of humanity is lost without a shred of righteousness that would permit God to accept any individual, at least on his own merit. He said, *"Therefore by the deeds of the law there shall no flesh be justified in His sight"* (Rom. 3:20). Yet, God has determined to bring mankind a salvation that necessarily involves sinners becoming righteous in His sight. This, Paul explained, is accomplished in the death of Christ, which was a sacrifice of atonement. Through faith in His blood, the individual who believes is declared righteous. Thus, salvation and righteousness come through faith in Jesus and what He did for us at the Cross; and through faith, salvation and righteousness are available to all.

There was a time on earth when in the book of heaven
An old account was standing for sins yet unforgiven;
My name was at the top, and many things below;
I went unto the Keeper, and settled long ago.

DIVINE *Healing*

CHAPTER 4

FAITH

FAITH

IN ROMANS 4, PAUL argues that faith is the same today as it was when it was exercised by Old Testament saints such as Abraham and David. Also, faith has the same result. Abraham and David won forgiveness by faith (Rom. 4:1-8), and for us today, forgiveness is also found by faith. We see in Romans, 4 that to believe means simply to count on God's promises. We accept the Word of God (God spoke), and in doing so, we accept God Himself.

Paul shows that the God, who spoke with promise to Abraham, is the same God who, in Jesus, speaks with promise to us: The God in *"whom he* (Abraham) *believed, even God, who quickens the dead, and calls those things which be not as though they were"* (Rom. 4:17). In Romans 4:18-25, Paul further defines faith. Here he analyzes Abraham's faith. Abraham faced the fact of his and Sarah's advanced age. He knew this meant that conceiving a child was impossible, but Abraham *"staggered not at the promise of God through unbelief; but was strong in faith, giving glory to God."* Instead, he was *"fully persuaded*

that, what He (God) *had promised, He was able also to perform."*
And so, Paul concludes, *"Therefore it was imputed to him for
righteousness"* (Rom. 4:20-22).

THE PROMISE

Abraham heard the promise. He looked beyond the
impossibility of its fulfillment and considered God. Confi-
dent that God would keep His promise, Abraham accepted
that what God announced would come to pass. The promise
Abraham believed was the promise that he would father a child.

God has delivered Jesus up for our sins and raised Him
to life again for our justification. The promise held out today
in the gospel in which we are to believe is the promise that
God will save us because of Jesus and His atoning work at the
Cross and our faith in that finished work. We look beyond
the impossibility that the natural person sees. We consider
God, and we, too, are convinced that what God has announced
will come to pass. Believing, we receive the gifts of salvation
and righteousness.

MAINTAINING OUR SALVATION

In Galatians 3, Paul not only proclaims the necessity of faith
in Christ for one's salvation, but he argues that our relationship with the Lord is also maintained by faith. We are not to
attempt to live in fellowship with God by trying to keep the
law. Paul reminds us, *"The just* (righteous) *shall live by faith"*

(Gal. 3:11), and that refers to faith in Christ and His atoning work on Calvary's Cross.

Law is based on a contrary principle: Reliance on human activity and performance. It is not based on promise. Since we must relate to God through His promise rather than through His works, we must continue on by faith in our relationship with the Lord. We must hear the words of Scripture as promise, and we must rely on them as promise.

In his personal testimony, Paul says:

> *I am crucified with Christ* (as the foundation of all victory; Paul here takes us back to Romans 6:3-5): *nevertheless I live* (have new life); *yet not I* (not by my own strength and ability), *but Christ lives in me* (by virtue of my dying with Him on the Cross and being raised with Him in newness of life): *and the life which I now live in the flesh* (my daily walk before God) *I live by the faith of the Son of God* (the Cross is ever the object of my faith), *who loved me, and gave Himself for me* (which is the only way that I could be saved) (Gal. 2:20) (The Expositor's Study Bible).

TRUE FAITH

The life of faith is ours as we continue to count on God's word to us; however, we must remember that the faith which the Holy Spirit addresses is faith in Christ and what Christ did for us at the Cross. This we must ever understand. Faith without the Cross is faith that God will not honor. Faith in the Cross is that which God will always honor, and we must never forget that. We hear God's promises and believe that God will do in us all that He has spoken. As we live by faith, the righteousness of which the Bible speaks as being ours in God's sight gradually infuses our life and character, and we become righteous persons in fact and in deed. It is all by faith in Christ.

However, we must ever understand that faith in the Word of God, at least for it to be true faith, must be with the understanding that the entirety of the Bible, as stated, points to Christ and Him crucified. So, when we speak of making the Bible the object of our faith, it must be with that in mind. That which says too much concludes by saying nothing. So, when we speak of having faith in the Word of God, it must ever be with the understanding that the Word of God, as stated, points strictly to Christ and His atoning work. In a sense, this means that Christ and Him crucified must ever be the object of our faith—and is how our salvation is maintained.

IT ALL COMES BY FAITH

As we've already stated, in Romans 4 and 5, Paul tells us that salvation comes by faith, and, as well, victory over sin comes by faith. That speaks of Christ and His atoning work at the Cross. When we come to Romans 6, this chapter explains to us how we can maintain our salvation, and do so by ever understanding that it is the Cross of Christ and faith in that finished work that gives us power through the Holy Spirit to live the life we ought to live. Then and only then, *"Sin shall not have dominion over you"* (Rom. 6:14).

So, when the Holy Spirit through Paul tells us how to successfully live for the Lord (this is what Romans 6 is all about), He takes us straight to the Cross (Rom. 6:3-5). This means that the Cross of Christ must ever be the object of our faith.

LOOKING BACK AT FAITH

We find as we study the Word of God that the object of faith has differed somewhat down through the ages as it regards the culminating effect. While the end result is the same, which is the Cross, the method of getting there, as stated, has somewhat varied.

In different ages, God has spoken different words of promise; however, even though the direction at times would be slightly different, the actual object of faith was always Christ and the Cross.

At the very dawn of time and at the fall of man, God promised that a redeemer would come (Gen. 3:15). This set the stage for Christ and His Cross. In keeping with that promise, He promised to Abraham a son and multiplied descendants. To those under the law, there was the promise of blessing to accompany obedience. To us, there is the promise of cleansing and acceptance through Christ, to whom all the other promises pointed.

In each age, faith is man's response to the promise. In each age, faith is trusting oneself to the God who has spoken. In each age, faith is accepted by God in place of a righteousness that no human being had or could have, at least on his own.

THE NEW TESTAMENT

In the New Testament, to which the entirety of the Old pointed, we see with unmistakable clarity that it is through faith that God gives salvation and righteousness—faith in Christ and His finished work. It is in the New Testament that we see with unmistakable clarity that faith is a personal response to God and a complete commitment of ourselves to Him. There also we see that faith calls for a continuing relationship of response to Jesus' Word.

It is in the New Testament that we see with unmistakable clarity that faith transforms human beings and brings us a life that is eternal, which can be experienced now. Through faith we come into a relationship with God in which He commits Himself not simply to declare us righteous, but also to make us truly good persons after the example of Christ. This is done solely by faith in the sacrifice of Christ. Only then can the Holy Spirit work satisfactorily within our lives and develop His fruit. Trusting God is the heart and soul of the faith that centers in our Lord Jesus Christ and His atoning work.

CHRIST AND THE CROSS EVER
THE OBJECT OF OUR FAITH

The believer must be careful not to fall into the trap into which Abraham almost succumbed. Distraught and discouraged because the promised son had not yet appeared, and inasmuch as it seemed the obstacles were abundant, he began to gradually move his eyes from the giver to the gift. This is a danger for many believers.

In response to this, *"The word of the LORD came unto Abram in a vision, saying, Fear not, Abram: I am your shield, and your exceeding great reward"* (Gen. 15:1). In this passage, the Lord brings Abraham back to the correct position of faith. The believer must never allow himself, for whatever reason, to be pulled away from the giver to the gift. While it is certainly exceedingly important that the gift (the promised son) be brought into the world, still, the Lord, in essence, would tell the Patriarch, "It is not the gift, but rather My person who is 'your exceeding great reward.'"

The modern faith movement has fallen into the error in which Abraham found himself. Faith has become the object with many instead of the giver of faith. In so doing, the danger is always prevalent that God's Word will in turn be used against Himself—or at least, there is an attempt to do so. In other words, with faith solely as the object instead of Christ and the Cross, the believer automatically concludes that he knows the will of God in any and all situations. Thereby, he sets out to use his faith to bring about that which he desires instead of what God desires.

THE WRONG DIRECTION

Actually, this is what Satan attempted to get Christ to do respecting the temptations in the wilderness. Christ was hungry, so why not introduce His power to His need? It was a logical conclusion, at least in the manner in which Satan proposed it. There was nothing sinful in bread, and neither was there anything sinful in the Lord using His power accordingly, or so Satan suggested. And so, millions reason the same thing.

However, if Jesus had done so, He would have been using His power for His own betterment, which would have been stepping outside the will of God; consequently, He would say to Satan, *"It is written, Man shall not live by bread alone, but by every word that proceeds out of the mouth of God"* (Mat. 4:4).

So, to use faith as an object, i.e., in order to acquire things at random pleasure, is not the will of God at all. The object of faith must ever be the giver of faith, who is the Lord Jesus Christ, and His atoning work. While the gift is always important, such as the promised son to Abraham, still, as stated, the giver of that gift was the exceeding great reward and not the gift itself.

GO IN PEACE, AND BE WHOLE OF YOUR PLAGUE

The heading adds a new dimension to the entirety of this episode. This woman not only gained healing but salvation, as well, the word *peace* assures this. It spoke of the health of both body and soul. As such, the proclamation of salvation is beautifully given in just a few words. The peace spoken of refers to peace with God. As a result of the fall, man lost his peace with God. As a result of sin that entered, there was an enmity that intruded between God and man. Because of his disobedience that brought about this enmity, man was estranged from God (Rom. 8:7; Eph. 2:15-16).

This lack of peace presents a troubled soul to the individual, which expresses itself in many ways, all of them adverse, whether physical, mental, domestic, or above all, spiritual. Such flows from a twisted human nature. It can only be assuaged by Christ as faith is evidenced in Him, as exampled by the woman who touched the hem of His garment.

PEACE AND THE CROSS

Jesus said, *"Peace I leave with you, My peace I give unto you: not as the world gives, give I unto you. Let not your heart be troubled, neither let it be afraid"* (Jn. 14:27). He then said, *"These things I have spoken unto you, that in Me you might have peace. In the world you shall have tribulation: but be of good cheer; I have overcome the world"* (Jn. 16:33).

The great word given by Christ to His disciples, as recorded in John 14:27, is all made possible by the Cross. The bearer of everything the Lord gives us is always the Holy Spirit (Jn. 16:14-15). In fact, every single thing that the Lord gives us, irrespective of what it might be, all and without exception is made possible by the Cross (Eph. 2:13-18).

The Cross of Christ took away all sin, which means that it atoned for all sin. Upon that being done, hostility caused by sin was forever removed. Now, the believer can *"come boldly unto the throne of grace, that we may obtain mercy, and find grace to help in time of need"* (Heb. 4:16).

BUT WHAT ABOUT BEFORE THE CROSS?

The sacrifice of clean animals at that time served as a stopgap measure until the time of the Cross one might say. In effect, it could be said that the Lord did on credit what He did with people at that time as it regarded miracles, healing, or whatever. He knew the Cross would pay the coming debt, and so He did things, as we've already said, on credit. However, let the reader understand the following:

- Jesus Christ is the source of everything that we receive from God (Jn. 1:1-3, 14, 29; 14:6).
- While Jesus is the source, the Cross of Christ is the means by which all of this is done (Rom. 6:3-14; I Cor. 1:17-18, 23; 2:2). The statement that the Cross is the means by which all of this is done is very important. If the believer doesn't understand that, such unbelief will greatly hinder us receiving from the Lord.
- With Jesus as the source and the Cross as the means, then the Cross of Christ must be the object of our faith. Of course, we aren't speaking of the wooden beam on which Jesus died, but rather what He there accomplished. Actually, what He did at the Cross makes everything possible (Col. 2:10-15; Gal. 6:14).
- With Christ as the source and the Cross as the means, and the only means, and with our faith anchored securely in Christ and the Cross, the Holy Spirit will then begin to work mightily on our behalf. However,

the Holy Spirit works only and entirely from the parameters of the Cross of Christ (Rom. 8:1-11; Eph. 2:13-18).

I have read book after book on the great subjects of the Bible. While the writers capably portray the problem, they never really give the solution to the problem. I suppose it's because they don't know the solution. The solution is, has always been, and shall always be Jesus Christ and Him crucified. That's why Paul said, *"we preach Christ crucified"* (I Cor. 1:23).

SANCTIFYING PEACE

There is a vast difference between justifying peace, which every single believer in the world has, and sanctifying peace. Justifying peace is the peace that comes to the new believer upon the born-again experience. At that moment, all hostility between God and the believing sinner is removed by virtue of what Christ did at the Cross and the faith of the believing sinner expressed in that finished work (Jn. 3:16).

However, the peace that Jesus mentioned in John 14:27 and John 16:33 is sanctifying peace. This is the type of peace that Paul addressed in almost all of his salutations to his epistles. For instance, he said to the Galatians, *"Grace be to you and peace from God the Father, and from our Lord Jesus Christ."* This is sanctifying peace.

Concerning this, Paul said, *"Who gave Himself for our sins* (the Cross), *that He might deliver us from this present evil world, according to the will of God and our Father"* (Gal. 1:3-4).

All believers have justifying peace and have such in the same capacity; however, the capacity of sanctifying peace is altogether different in different believers. In other words, some will have sanctifying peace to a far greater degree than others.

THE BLOOD

As an example, when the Lord told Moses to tell the children of Israel that He was going to pass through the land of Egypt that night, and every home that didn't have the blood applied to the doorposts, the firstborn in that home would die, it was, to say the least, a chilling announcement.

More than likely, there were some Israelites who went to bed that night and slept soundly, totally trusting in what the Lord had said, because they had applied the blood to the doorposts as the Lord commanded. Therefore, they rested calmly and serenely. On the other hand, there were undoubtedly some of the children of Israel who, even though the blood was applied to the doorposts, still spent the night in anxiety and fear.

Irrespective, even though there was anxiety and fear in their hearts that robbed them of peace that particular night, still, they were just as safe as the person who slept soundly. As well, the person who slept soundly was just as safe as the one who walked the floor all night long with anxiety and fear. The one who slept soundly had sanctifying peace, while the one who did not sleep at all but walked the floor all night long had no sanctifying peace whatsoever. However, he still was saved because the blood had been applied to the doorposts.

HOW CAN THE BELIEVER HAVE
SANCTIFYING PEACE?

First of all, let's state that it is impossible for the unbeliever to have any type of sanctifying peace. That should be obvious. However, the believer can have sanctifying peace, no matter the problem and no matter the difficulty, if he or she will only carry out the following: Going back to the deliverance of the children of Israel from Egyptian bondage, the degree of peace on that fateful night pertained to the degree of faith in the blood applied to the doorpost. The Lord had said, *"When I see the blood, I will pass over you"* (Ex. 12:13). It is the same presently.

As a believer, you are to place your faith exclusively in Christ and the Cross, as we've already stated. You must trust totally and completely in what He has done for you and not allow your faith to be moved from Christ and the Cross to something else. If you do that, and you continue to do that, the Holy Spirit will guarantee your peace.

As we've stated, this sanctifying peace doesn't guarantee an absence of all problems, difficulties, and troubles; however, it does guarantee a peace in the midst of all of those troubles.

THE GARMENT OF PRAISE

A short time back, the Lord gave me something that's been a lifesaver, and it's so wonderful and good that I want everyone else to have it.

Nearly 2,800 years ago, the great prophet Isaiah said, *"To appoint unto them who mourn in Zion, to give unto them beauty for ashes, the oil of joy for mourning, the garment of praise for the spirit of heaviness; that they might be called trees of righteousness, the planting of the LORD, that He might be glorified"* (Isa. 61:3).

I want to call your attention to one phrase in the entirety of this Scripture, *"The garment of praise for the spirit of heaviness."*

Before I explain this, please let me make some preliminary remarks.

First of all, when the Bible mentions the heart, it isn't speaking of the organ in a person's chest that beats 72 to 80 times a minute. It is speaking of something else entirely. I think one can say that it is speaking of the soul and the spirit of man, in other words, the real you. And so, Jesus said that all sin begins in the heart (Mat. 15:19). So, if the heart is not the physical organ in our physical bodies, what exactly was Jesus talking about?

He was actually saying that sin begins in the spirit of the soul of man. Some Bible scholars even say that the mind is a part of the heart of which Jesus spoke. At any rate, before sin can lodge in the soul and the spirit of man, it must first have its beginning in the mind. Once it is conceived in the mind, it then goes to the soul and the spirit and then is committed (that is, if it is committed) by the physical body.

That's what Paul was talking about when he said: *"Neither yield you your members* (of your mortal body) *as instruments of unrighteousness unto sin* (the sin nature)*: but yield yourselves unto God* (we are to yield ourselves to Christ and the Cross;

that alone guarantees victory over the sin nature), *as those who are alive from the dead* (we have been raised with Christ in 'newness of life'), *and your members* (the physical members of your physical body) *as instruments of righteousness unto God"* (Rom. 6:13).

So, we have to find a way to counteract the seed of sin fomenting in our minds. How do we do that?

THE MIND OF MAN

It is impossible to think on two things at one time. We may think we can do that, but we really can't. Whatever we are thinking, as fleeting as it might be, still is all that we're thinking about at the moment.

The following is what the Holy Spirit meant when He gave to Isaiah the short phrase, *"The garment of praise for the spirit of heaviness"*: As a believer, when thoughts of the Lord come to your mind in any manner, instantly begin to praise the Lord. You don't have to do it out loud.

Actually, you can do it under your breath, but praise the Lord, which permeates your soul, your spirit, your mind, i.e., the heart. Just tell the Lord under your breath how much you love Him, and how you thank Him for all the wonderful things He does for you. You can even praise Him in the spirit. In a few moments' time, your mind will go to something else. If you will do what I've said every time your mind goes to the Lord, you will find that fear will be dispelled, evil thoughts will be dispelled, and doubt and unbelief will be thrown aside, while a feeling of well-being will flood your soul. Do it constantly, never stopping.

I do believe that this will keep back much sickness. It is God's preventive medicine one might say.

THE SPIRIT OF HEAVINESS

The spirit of heaviness is spiritual oppression and emanates from spirits of darkness. It drags the physical body down, and again, causes much sickness and emotional disturbances. However, when you begin to praise the Lord, and do it constantly, every time your mind goes to the Lord, you will find that spirit of heaviness, which takes many forms, leaving entirely with nothing left but praises for the Lord. As stated, this is God's medicine; this is His security that He gives to us.

The Holy Spirit knew exactly what He was saying when He gave the word *"garment of praise"* to Isaiah so long, long ago. We are to wear the praises of the Lord as a garment exactly as I have tried to tell you. That means that the barbs of Satan cannot get through and cannot be given any place at all and, therefore, must remain silent.

If you will do what I've said do, and what I've tried my best to outline to you, I think you will find situations improving, fear being dispelled, and a feeling of joy and euphoria filling your heart. Try it; it doesn't cost anything.

And remember this, every victory we have and every good thing that comes to us from the Lord—and every good thing does come from Him—are all made possible by the Cross of Christ. There Satan was totally and completely defeated, along with every demon spirit and other fallen angels. It is the Cross of Christ that makes it all possible.

WHOLENESS OF MIND, BODY, AND SPIRIT

From the phrase, *"Go in peace, and be whole of your plague,"* one can make an excellent scriptural case that healing for the body, as well as salvation of the soul, is a part of the atonement, i.e., the price that Jesus paid at Calvary. Man cannot be whole unless he is whole in every capacity. To argue that the atonement only included salvation from sin is a failure not only to understand the total fall of man but, also, a failure to understand the total redemption of man by Christ at Calvary. Man is either totally redeemed, made whole in every respect, or not redeemed at all! Of course, we know that Jesus redeemed the whole man.

Let us say it another way: There's no such thing as a partial justification by faith. One is either totally justified or not justified at all.

To argue that because Christians still get sick, healing was not included in the atonement is to argue that salvation from sin is not in the atonement because Christians still sin at times. In truth, the total redemption of man in the atonement, including both spiritual and physical, and financial, as well, is not affected by the fact of either continued sin or sickness. However, the entirety of the salvation process, as provided at Calvary, is not yet completed as far as results are concerned, even though it is completed as far as the fact is concerned.

FIRSTFRUITS

Concerning this very thing, Paul said, *"But ourselves also, which have the firstfruits of the Spirit, even we ourselves groan within ourselves, waiting for the adoption, to wit, the redemption of our body"* (Rom. 8:23). As the apostle said, we presently only have the firstfruits of the Spirit as it regards all that Jesus did in the atonement. The balance will be received at the resurrection when this physical body will be redeemed—exchanged one might say, in effect, for a glorified body. Then the totality of what Jesus paid for at the Cross will be completely realized.

The believer has presently been sanctified and justified *"in the name of the Lord Jesus, and by the Spirit of our God"* (I Cor. 6:11). However, the believer has not yet been glorified, which will take place at the first resurrection of life. This will then, and for all time, complete the salvation process. Then sin and sickness will no longer be possible (Rom. 8:17-25; I Cor. 15:51-54).

"While He yet spoke, there came from the ruler of the synagogue's house certain which said, Your daughter is dead: why troublest the Master any further?" (Mk. 5:35).

WHILE HE YET SPOKE

The heading refers to someone coming from the home of Jairus and bringing a message, even while the Lord was speaking to the woman who had just been healed. The message would not be good.

But yet, if Jesus is speaking, good and wonderful things always happen. If not, it's because of unbelief. We will find that when He does speak to the ruler of the synagogue, it will be words of hope and words of life.

THERE CAME FROM THE RULER OF THE SYNAGOGUE'S HOUSE CERTAIN WHICH SAID, YOUR DAUGHTER IS DEAD

One might well imagine the terrible blow that Jairus suffered when he heard the words, *"Your daughter is dead."* He was, no doubt, very pleased at the healing of this dear woman, but at the same time, his heart was breaking for his little daughter. He must have been extremely concerned regarding the delay brought about by the healing of the woman. Jesus' searching for her after her healing and the time it took for her to give her testimony must have caused terrible anxiety in the heart of this man. And now, he received the worst message of all, confirming his fears: *"Your daughter is dead."*

WHY DO YOU TROUBLE THE MASTER ANY FURTHER?

The heading proclaims the end of their faith, at least those who had brought the disconcerting message. I think the next verse proclaims that Jairus also felt that it was now too late.

However, with God, it's never too late. Man quickly comes to the end of his resources, but God never comes to the end of His. My grandmother taught me when I was a child, "Jimmy, God is a big God, so ask big." That simple statement has helped me to touch this world for Christ. She taught me to ask big, and thank God she did.

All of this meant that nothing is impossible with God, and I mean nothing. What Jesus will now do proves the situation.

"As soon as Jesus heard the word that was spoken, He said unto the ruler of the synagogue, Be not afraid, only believe" (Mk. 5:36).

In effect, Jesus said, "Stop fearing and be believing."

AS SOON AS JESUS HEARD THE WORD THAT WAS SPOKEN

The heading means that Jesus overheard what was being said.

We learn from all of this that God can do anything, and when we say anything, we mean anything.

What did Jesus hear?

He heard that the little girl, who, incidentally, was 12 years old, had died. In a sense, as well, He could hear the broken heart of Jairus.

HE SAID UNTO THE RULER OF THE SYNAGOGUE

According to the statement given by Christ, upon the news of the death of his daughter, Jairus had ceased to believe.

However, before we criticize him, would we have done any better?

He had believed that Jesus could definitely heal his daughter, but now that the child was dead?

Man can only go so far with his faith, and now Jairus had traveled that distance. He could not really see at that time what Jesus could do inasmuch as the child was dead. But then he heard something that sounded strange to his ears.

BE NOT AFRAID, ONLY BELIEVE

This phrase constituted some of the greatest words that Jairus would ever hear, but yet, completely beyond his comprehension. In effect, Jesus said, "Stop fearing" and "be believing," meaning to continue believing, even in the presence of death. What a valuable lesson this should be to all!

To believe is one thing, but to continue to believe, even in the face of extremely adverse circumstances, as here proclaimed, is the key to receiving what we want from the Lord. At what level does our faith weaken and die? The Lord is ever seeking to strengthen our faith, which is always done through the Word of God (Rom. 10:17). This simply means that we are to believe the Word of God, and to believe it despite the circumstances.

I am convinced that the more mature one is in Christ, the more the Lord allows circumstances to build, which, at times, make the situation even more impossible. I believe He does this in order that our faith may be increased by trusting solely in God's Word.

The idea is that we walk by faith, not by sight (II Cor. 5:7). Consequently, the Lord will allow the sight to be increased by adverse circumstances, difficulties, and even impossibilities. Because of their loud clamor it becomes very easy to look at these things. The secret is to keep one's eye and heart on the Word despite the circumstances or difficulties.

I think the difficulties could not be any worse than recorded here, with the child actually having died. And yet, Jesus said to him, "Don't fear, keep believing." He says the same to us, as well.

"And He suffered no man to follow Him, save Peter, and James, and John the brother of James" (Mk. 5:37).

PETER, JAMES, AND JOHN

Why these three—Peter, James, and John?

This is the first of three occasions when Jesus singles them out from the other disciples:

- At the raising of the girl from the dead, Jesus would portray to these three His power.
- At the transfiguration, only these three were allowed to witness this event (Mk. 9:1-2). Here, He showed them His glory.
- During His passion in the garden of Gethsemane, likewise, only the three were allowed (Mk. 14:32-35). Here, He showed them His sufferings.

The only answer for these three being included, with the others excluded from these momentous occasions, is that the three showed by their actions that they desired a closer walk with Him. I am aware of no other explanation. Those who *"hunger and thirst after righteousness"* are filled (Mat. 5:6). Consequently, it stands to reason that they who hunger and thirst the more are filled the more.

"And He came to the house of the ruler of the synagogue, and seeing the tumult, and them who wept and wailed greatly" (Mk. 5:38).

AND HE CAME TO THE HOUSE OF
THE RULER OF THE SYNAGOGUE

What was in the mind of Jairus all the time they were on the way to his house? Did he really realize what Jesus was about to do? It seems from Luke 7:11 that this was not the first occasion of Jesus raising one from the dead, although that chronology is not confirmed.

When Jesus comes to the house, any house, things are instantly made better, the impossible made possible, death turned to life, little turned to much, etc.

What kind of God do you serve? The God we are supposed to serve is a God of miracles. We must understand that and believe that simply because it is true.

AND SEEING THE TUMULT

The heading speaks to the activity of the paid mourners and Jesus examining their actions with a critical and careful eye.

In all of this, we will see the terrible unbelief of the human heart. This tumult had no real sincerity and was simply for show.

AND THEM WHO WEPT AND WAILED GREATLY

This had to do with the practice and custom of that time of hiring mourners to do this thing. Their mourning was not real, but fake. Most of them probably didn't even know the child.

As the next verse portrays, the actions of Christ proclaim the fact that He was not in sympathy with such activity.

Even though it was then a custom, I cannot see how that such even remotely bettered any situation of this nature. What good would it do to have someone shout and holler and wail greatly, especially considering that it was all fake, and that they did not even really know the little girl?

"And when He was come in, He said unto them, Why do you make this ado, and weep? the damsel is not dead, but sleeps" (Mk. 5:39).

AND WHEN HE WAS COME IN

This did not mean that she was actually not dead, but that the child was not dead to stay dead. As well, the word *sleeps* brings us to the fact of the resurrection. In the Scriptures, the believing dead are constantly referred to as sleeping; however, it is only the body that sleeps, with the soul and the spirit at death instantly going to be with Christ, that is, if the person is saved.

The heading refers to Jesus entering into the midst of the paid mourners. Jairus, Peter, James, and John were with Him. To be sure, despite the unbelief of these paid mourners, He would quickly change this situation from terrible hurt and pain to that of life and joy. Death cannot remain death in His presence. It actually seems that every single funeral that Christ met in His earthly sojourn, He quickly changed it to a family reunion, and did so by raising the dead.

HE SAID UNTO THEM, WHY DO YOU MAKE THIS ADO, AND WEEP?

His question refers to all the uproar and constant wailing. As stated, the Lord was not in sympathy with this custom and practice, and for all the obvious reasons. It did not help anyone, and, in fact, it only increased the terrible grief and pain.

THE DAMSEL IS NOT DEAD, BUT SLEEPS

As we have stated, this statement given by Christ did not mean that the girl was not actually dead, but that the child was not dead to stay dead. Some false cults teach soul-sleep, meaning that at death the soul sleeps until the resurrection, etc. Such is not taught in Scripture. All the Scriptures used by these cults clearly refer to the body, which does sleep in the dust of the earth until the resurrection of the body (Dan. 12:2; Jn. 5:28-29; I Cor., Chpt. 15).

The body is the only part of man that dies at physical death (James 2:26). The reason it dies is because the inner man, the soul and spirit, the life of the body, leaves the body. The body then goes back to dust and is spoken of as being asleep (Gen. 3:19; Eccl. 3:19-21; Mat. 9:24; Jn. 11:11; I Cor. 11:30; 15:6, 18-20, 51; I Thess. 4:13-17).

Some may ask as to what kind of body we will have in the resurrection. The Scripture tells us that it will be a glorified body.

During the time of Paul, some were ridiculing Paul's teaching concerning the resurrection, and especially the resurrection of the dead body. Paul answered them very quickly. He said: *"But some man will say, How are the dead raised up? and with what body do they come? You fool, that which you sow is not quickened, except it die … But God gives it a body as it has pleased Him, and to every seed his own body"* (I Cor. 15:35-36, 38).

In other words, the Lord is not going to try to rehabilitate the old body we had before death, but is going to give us a brand new body, a glorified body.

Paul also said, *"It is sown a natural body; it is raised a spiritual body"* (I Cor. 15:44). I might quickly add that our glorified bodies will be like His (I Jn. 3:2).

"And they laughed Him to scorn. But when He had put them all out, He took the father and the mother of the damsel, and them who were with Him, and entered in where the damsel was lying" (Mk. 5:40).

AND THEY LAUGHED HIM TO SCORN

This refers to their weeping suddenly turning to laughing. I think it now becomes obvious why Jesus was opposed to this custom. Moreover, their deriding and jeering were at Him! They were not content to merely disagree with Him about the child being dead, but they felt they must loudly proclaim their disagreement by jeering Him.

BUT WHEN HE HAD PUT THEM ALL OUT

The heading presents a strong statement, meaning that He had to use pressure to make these individuals leave. It was somewhat akin to the forceful ejection when He cleansed the temple. There is no evidence that it went quite that far, but very close to it!

HE TOOK THE FATHER AND THE MOTHER OF THE DAMSEL, AND THEM WHO WERE WITH HIM

The group refers to Jairus, his wife, Peter, James, and John.

AND ENTERED IN WHERE THE DAMSEL WAS LYING

The word *entered* actually refers to a person going on a journey even though only a few feet, at least in this instance. It conveyed the idea of distance even though only a short piece. In effect, it pointed forward to the coming resurrection.

Wuest says, "That the word was chosen because it conveyed the idea of distance. Even though it was only a few feet from this room to where the child was lying dead, what would transpire, the raising of the child from the dead, would portray a journey of incomprehensible proportions. All would be taken to a dimension of faith and power that are impossible in the natural sense."

"And He took the damsel by the hand, and said unto her, Talitha cumi; which is, being interpreted, Damsel, I say unto you, arise" (Mk. 5:41).

AND HE TOOK THE DAMSEL BY THE HAND

The heading refers to a strong grip. What were the thoughts of Jairus and the girl's mother when Jesus reached down and took her hand?

AND SAID UNTO HER, TALITHA CUMI

This was spoken in Aramaic, the same tongue used concerning our Lord's words on the Cross, *"My God, My God, why have You forsaken Me?"* As the original language was reported in these two cases, quite possibly they relate to each other. As Jesus defeated death at the home of Jairus, likewise, and for the whole world, He defeated death at Calvary.

The actual statement means, "Little girl, I say to you, arise." Consequently, it means that Mark gave us the original language in which Jesus spoke the word.

"And straightway the damsel arose, and walked; for she was of the age of twelve years. And they were astonished with a great astonishment" (Mk. 5:42).

AND STRAIGHTWAY THE DAMSEL AROSE, AND WALKED

While the Scriptures only record three people being raised from the dead by Christ, Augustine says that He raised many more, which He, no doubt, did.

The heading means that the girl immediately arose upon the command of Christ and began to walk about the room, possibly to her mother and father, and then maybe even to Christ.

FOR SHE WAS OF THE AGE OF TWELVE YEARS

This simply relates her age.

What her sickness had been that had caused her death, we are not told; however, whatever it was, she no longer had it.

AND THEY WERE ASTONISHED WITH A GREAT ASTONISHMENT

The heading means they were simply amazed beyond words. Peter, James, and John, along with the mother and father, stood there as if in a trance, knowing that what they had seen was true. Yet, they were hardly able to believe it.

As someone has said, "He raised the dead then to show that He will be able to raise the dead on that resurrection morn!"

"And He charged them straitly that no man should know it; and commanded that something should be given her to eat" (Mk. 5:43).

AND HE CHARGED THEM STRAITLY
THAT NO MAN SHOULD KNOW IT

They must not relate the account of this miracle. There were reasons for this, the least not being the furor that religious leaders would cause, but it is certain that such news could not be kept.

Actually, His command was probably futile inasmuch as the paid mourners knew what He had proposed to do, and certainly the very appearance of the child would prove beyond the shadow of a doubt that He had done it—raised her from the dead. So, even though they were charged *"straitly,"* i.e., with insistence, still, it is doubtful that the secret was kept for very long.

AND COMMANDED THAT SOMETHING
SHOULD BE GIVEN HER TO EAT

Jesus' statement could have been in reference to her past illness. Possibly food had exacerbated whatever problem she had. Nevertheless, if that was the problem, it no longer was, and she could now eat anything she desired.

This chapter encompasses the former maniac of Gadara being commanded to go into the gospel field (v. 19); the woman, to go into peace (v. 34); and the child, to go into dinner (v. 43). These three commands, in reverse order, apply to all who have experienced the saving grace and power of Christ. The Bible must be their food; assurance of salvation, their experience; and preaching the gospel, their employment.

Williams said, "All Christians, honorably earning their bread, should regard preaching the gospel, at least in some way, as their main business."

Standing on the promises of Christ my King
Through eternal ages, let His praises ring
Glory, hallelujah, I will shout and sing,
Standing on the promises of God.

DIVINE
Healing

MIRACLE OF
MIRACLES

MIRACLE OF MIRACLES

"THEN JESUS WENT THENCE, and departed into the coasts of Tyre and Sidon" (Mat. 15:21).

THEN JESUS WENT THENCE

The heading portrays Jesus leaving probably Capernaum and going to the borders of Tyre and Sidon.

These two cities were located on the Mediterranean Sea north of Israel. Both are very prominent in Old Testament history.

The Scripture does not say that Jesus went into these cities but merely to the border between Israel and Lebanon where they were located.

These two areas of Tyre and Sidon were steeped in heathenistic idol worship. Their gods were Baal and Ashtaroth, which they, in one form or the other, continued to worship even during the time of Christ.

Coming back to the present, as invited guests of Israel, Frances and I, along with Donnie and others, had the opportunity to go into Lebanon to tape a television special. This was during the heaviest fighting of the war in which Israel attempted to expunge the Palestinians from Lebanon because of their constantly lobbing of rockets over into Israel. It was quite an experience.

The present border between Israel and Lebanon, which possibly is very near the location where it was in Jesus' day, is actually a very beautiful place.

Here the cliffs rise up from the Mediterranean. As well, the altitude rises somewhat as the topography changes to a mountainous district.

LEBANON

As we crossed the border that day, Israeli soldiers were everywhere. There were long lines of trucks backed up that were coming from Lebanon. They were bringing back all types of burned out and destroyed Russian equipment that had been taken from the Palestinians and the Syrians.

As we stopped at the border for the regular regulation ritual, I had the occasion to stand there for a length of time, looking out over the Mediterranean, as well as back into Israel. Almost immediately below our feet at the bottom of the mountain were gigantic caves that opened up to the sea. We learned a short time later that the Israelis had located huge quantities of weapons and ammunition that had been stored there by the Palestinians.

The closest Jewish town to the border is Nahariyya. It is a resort area with a population between 10 and 20,000. We spent the night there just before going into Lebanon.

I do not know if that little city even existed during the time of Christ; however, I do know that somewhere close to there, and possibly that very place, Christ came. Consequently, one of the greatest miracles recorded in the Bible took place there.

To be sure, within itself, it was no greater than many of the other miracles of Christ. However, the manner in which it took place provides a tremendous lesson for all Bible students.

"And, behold, a woman of Canaan came out of the same coasts, and cried unto Him, saying, Have mercy on me, O Lord, thou Son of David; my daughter is grievously vexed with a devil" (Mat. 15:22).

AND, BEHOLD, A WOMAN OF CANAAN CAME OUT OF THE SAME COASTS

The two words, *"And, behold,"* mark the sudden intrusion of this woman into the mission of Christ. When Matthew wrote these words, no doubt, the Holy Spirit moved upon him to say them as he did in order to highlight this unexpected turn of events.

The heading concludes her to be a Gentile. Mark called her a Greek and a Syrophoenician.

At any rate, the phrase, *"A woman of Canaan,"* says it all. She was an *"alien(s) from the commonwealth of Israel, and strangers* (a stranger) *from the covenants of promise, having no hope, and without God in the world"* (Eph. 2:12). As such, she was typical of all Gentiles and epitomized you who hold this book in your hands.

Her life was one of idol worship, and a cruel worship it was, even employing human sacrifice.

Whether human sacrifices continued unto the time of Christ is not known, but in centuries past, they had been rampant.

How this woman heard of Jesus is not known. No doubt, His fame had spread to this part of the world, and the stories abounded of the tremendous miracles He was performing. Now He was close to her home. It would be the greatest day in her life. If He had not come to this area, she would never have had the privilege of knowing Him or of experiencing the tremendous deliverance afforded her daughter.

As well, there is a great possibility that the Holy Spirit had our Lord to go to this place simply because of this woman.

WORLD EVANGELISM

This illustration speaks to me of the dire necessity of taking the gospel of Jesus Christ to the world. Paul would later say, *"How then shall they call on Him in whom they have not believed? and how shall they believe in Him of whom they have not heard? and how shall they hear without a preacher"* (Rom. 10:14)?

That is the reason we labor day and night at Jimmy Swaggart Ministries to take this gospel to the world. World evangelism is my calling. I live it, breathe it, and seek to carry it out with every fiber of my being.

As well, that is the reason for the SonLife Broadcasting Network, which is being aired all over the world 24 hours a day, seven days a week. We feel that we have the message, which is the Message of the Cross. This is not something new. Actually, it is the gospel (I Cor. 1:17). As we have stated, Jesus Christ is the new covenant, and the Cross of Christ is the meaning of that covenant. This meaning was given to the apostle Paul, which he gave to us in his 14 epistles.

Every single believer is responsible for helping to take the gospel to the world. None is excluded! All are commanded to be involved in this work—the preachers and the laity alike (Mk. 16:15).

Every person in the world has the right to hear the gospel. Now more than ever, due to the advent of television, the opportunity presents itself to reach most of the world with the great and glorious gospel of Jesus Christ, and to do so in a short period of time. To be sure, each one of us will be held responsible for our part in this task.

WHAT KIND OF GOSPEL?

That's the question!

If the right gospel is not presented, which is the gospel of Jesus Christ, then whatever it is that is presented is of no value whatsoever, but rather will do great harm. That's the tragedy! The gospel of Jesus Christ can be said to be Jesus Christ and Him crucified. Most of what is presently given to the world that passes for gospel is no gospel at all. At this ministry, we have seen literally hundreds of thousands (I exaggerate not) brought to a saving knowledge of Jesus Christ because the right gospel has been presented under and by the anointing of the Holy Spirit. I speak of television aired all over the world and giant citywide crusades conducted in various cities of the world.

GET IT DONE

On July 1, 1985, on a Monday morning, that is, if I remember the day correctly, the Lord gave me a vision of the coming harvest.

In those days, it was my custom to drive my car close to a railroad track that was about a mile from our house. I would sit in the car and study the Word for a short period of time and then spend some time in prayer while walking down the track. Then it was a place of solitude and was actually very beautiful. Now it's full of businesses and houses.

At any rate, I had no inkling that morning of what the Lord would do; however, as I started walking down the track while seeking the Lord, all of a sudden the scene around me changed. Across the horizon in every direction were cotton fields. The stalks were so heavily laden with cotton that there was no room for leaves or anything else. As stated, it stretched over the horizon in every direction.

I marveled at the tremendous harvest, and then I noted a couple of mechanical pickers in the distance. Then, to my left out of the east, I saw it. It was a storm that was coming, with the heavens jet black. I instantly knew that if the harvest wasn't gathered quickly, it would be totally lost. I also knew that it would not be possible for those two mechanical pickers to make any headway.

THE WORD OF THE LORD

About that time, I reached the place to where I normally turned around and went back to the car, and then the Lord spoke to my heart.

He said to me, "I want you to place the telecast in every city in the world that will accept it." Then He said, "I will hold back the storm for a period of time until it can be done."

Then the Lord said something else: "While I have called others for different localities around the world, I have called this ministry alone (Jimmy Swaggart Ministries) for the entirety of the world. So, don't fail Me."

I did everything that I could do to carry out that command, but circumstances arose that made it impossible for me to make any headway. It broke my heart a thousand times over, but there was nothing more I could do. We did see some tremendous things done, such as the telecast airing over the former Soviet Union, which saw over a million people brought to a saving knowledge of Jesus Christ. That figure comes from the number of letters that we received during that three-year span.

THE COMMISSION

Then, on one particular afternoon in 2014 when I went to prayer, I little knew that afternoon what the Lord would do. At a point in time, the Lord took me back through the vision all over again. I saw it just as real as I had seen it that day in 1985, and then the Lord spoke to my heart, and graphically so.

He said, "The commission that I gave you July 1, 1985, that Monday morning is still in force." Then He said, "Get it done."

I have no way to properly explain just exactly how I felt. I couldn't believe what I was feeling and sensing. The commission was still in force? How could it be? However, I knew beyond the shadow of a doubt that the Lord had spoken. That's why we drive everything so hard—we must get it done. That's why we are airing television all over the world. This is what God has called us to do, and we must do it.

Let me give you a personal testimony regarding what happened in the former Soviet Union when we began to air the telecast in all 14 of those Soviet Republics. In fact, the telecast was aired each week over TV-1 out of Moscow, which went into every single part of the Soviet Union.

Actually, there were 7,000 repeater stations scattered all over that vast area—the largest land mass in the world. Through the preaching of the gospel by the means of television, we saw a harvest of souls that was absolutely phenomenal to say the least. Again, we give the Lord all the praise and all the glory. Let me give you a personal experience that came out of that great harvest.

A PERSONAL EXPERIENCE

Sometime ago, I received a telephone call from a pastor friend who related to me a beautiful testimony. He had just returned from Moscow, where he and other preachers from America had conducted a week-long teaching seminar, to which they had brought in Russian pastors from all over the former Soviet Union. He explained to me that they did this once a year, even paying the expenses of these pastors to get them to Moscow.

Considering that most of these pastors in the former Soviet Union had very little Bible training, this, of course, was an extremely valuable time for them.

During the course of one of the teaching sessions, he happened to ask the roomful of pastors, numbering somewhat over 100, exactly how they had found Christ. Actually, he had each one stand and give a brief testimony to this all-important experience.

He said to me, "Brother Swaggart, how pleasantly surprised I was when over half of these pastors, some of them pastoring churches of over 1,000 in attendance, told how they had found Christ as a result of your telecast." He said, "I just had to call you and give you that bit of news."

AS IT HAPPENED

Believing that God was going to open the door in this vast land then known as the Soviet Union and that the Lord had told me to do so, we began to translate our television program from English to Russian. If I remember correctly, this was in 1987.

Jim Woolsey had been working for over a year to try and bring about this miracle of all miracles. But first, let me relate to you something that the Lord did, which told us what was going to happen in what was then the Soviet Union.

A WORD OF WISDOM

The year was 1986 if I remember correctly. Frances and I, along with Jim Woolsey and a missionary friend, went to Moscow for a series of meetings in what was then the Soviet Union. I preached in Moscow, in Siberia, and, as well, in Minsk, Belarus. It was in Belarus that the following took place.

It was a Sunday morning. We had traveled all night by train from Moscow, and I was to preach at a Baptist church and a Pentecostal church in that city. The Pentecostal church was jammed to capacity, and there was a tremendous spirit in the place. When I began to preach, I sensed an unusually heavy anointing.

I made a statement in the midst of the message, and the interpreter did not interpret it. In fact, he said nothing. He was standing a little bit behind me, and so I felt that possibly he didn't hear me. So, I made the statement again, but once again, he did not interpret it.

I turned around and looked at him, and tears were rolling down his face. Right there that Sunday morning, he gave his heart to Christ. He had been a KGB agent for a number of years, but that morning, his world changed.

After a few moments' time, he gathered his composure together and then began to interpret for me.

Right in the midst of the message, the Lord gave me a word of wisdom. I said: "The gospel of Jesus Christ is going to be proclaimed in every city, town, and village in the entirety of the Soviet Union." That was it, but what a statement!

When the service ended, and Frances and I were leaving, I turned to her and said, "Did you hear that which was stated about the gospel being ministered all over the Soviet Union?" She nodded in the affirmative and said, "Oh yes, I heard it."

I thought in my heart and mind, "How in the world could this be?" The Soviet Union was atheistic. They didn't believe there was a God, so how in the world could the gospel be proclaimed in every city, town, and village?

But, of course, the Holy Spirit knew exactly what He was doing, and to be sure, that word of wisdom (prophecy) was fulfilled to the letter. Let me tell you about it.

A MIRACLE OF MIRACLES

Jim Woolsey made some 30 trips to Moscow, trying to get Soviet television to air our program. Yes, I said 30 trips.

Finally, they consented. We first began to air in Riga, Latvia, a Soviet Republic. Actually, Moscow sent a KGB agent to Riga to inquire of the television station as to why they were airing our program. To my knowledge, it was the very first gospel program ever aired in the former Soviet Union. As stated, it was translated into Russian.

The station management, which, of course, was state controlled, informed the agent that they were airing it because it was what the people demanded. At any rate, even though the agent was very upset, the program was allowed to continue. In the meantime, Jim kept working with the main office of communication in Moscow, trying to get our television program on to cover the entire 14 republics of what was then the Soviet Union.

In 1990, we were then able to begin airing the telecast over TV-1 in Moscow. It had formerly been the major communist government network, which reached the entirety of all 14 Soviet Republics. It aired over some 7,000 repeater stations, covering some 300 million people.

THE MAIL

For nearly three years, we had a post office box in Moscow in order for the people to be able to write us if they so desired. In 1991, we received over a million letters even though we had told the people that we had no means to answer their letters, but that's how hungry they were for the gospel.

Considering the vastness of that area, television was the only way that one could quickly reach the masses. To be sure, that is what the Lord has called me to do. In all honesty, it would take hundreds, if not thousands, of Spirit-filled missionaries to reach that vast land, and even many years at that.

We were able to touch the entirety of that vast area in a very short period of time and with astounding results.

I will have to give Jim Woolsey the credit for having the faith to knock on that door until it finally opened. Of course, we give the Lord all the praise and glory for that which He helped us to do.

All over the world, there are multiple hundreds of millions of people just like this woman of Canaan. They must have the opportunity to hear the gospel and to know the Lord Jesus Christ. There is nothing more important than that!

AND CRIED UNTO HIM

As it concerns this woman of Canaan, the heading constitutes a message within itself.

The woman was desperate. She had come to receive something from Christ, and she would not leave without getting that which she asked.

Inasmuch as the word *cried* means "to clamor," or, in other words, "to speak with great emotion," the Holy Spirit through Matthew gives us an idea of her desperation and the cry of her heart. I daresay that if anyone will come to Christ in this manner, and I mean anyone, an answer will be forthcoming.

BIBLE FAITH

Too many people approach the Lord in a lackadaisical way, and most of the time, they receive nothing. To be sure, one is not advocating that the loudness of one's approach assures the answer, but this we do know: Bible faith will not be denied. There is always an urgency about faith that produces an emotion in the soul of the individual who comes to God. One can see this in the lives of the Bible greats, such as Abraham. In regard to the promise of God respecting the coming child, Isaac, Abraham felt the urgency so greatly to see the promise of God carried out in his life that he even attempted to help the Lord. This, of course, turned out to be catastrophic. Obviously, this was wrong, but nevertheless, it portrayed his feelings.

The apostle Paul is another example. There was an urgency about his ministry, his life, and his efforts. Faith produces such an urgency. As well, it produces an emotion as exampled by this woman of Canaan.

This dear lady did not really know God; however, she did know her need, and she did know who Jesus was, which is more than could be said of the religious leaders of Israel.

SAYING, HAVE MERCY ON ME, O LORD, THOU SON OF DAVID

The heading presents a petition to the Lord that was actually wrong in principle but right in faith.

As a minister of the circumcision for the truth of God to fulfill the promises made to the fathers, Christ refused to answer the Gentile petition addressed to Him as *"Son of David."* This was a Jewish statement as it pertained to Christ, and this Gentile had no right to use it as she did.

However, when the woman took the place of a "dog," thus admitting she had no claim, but rather was throwing herself on His mercy and grace as Lord, He responded at once. The Scripture says that He was so to act, that the Gentiles also may glorify God for His mercy (Rom. 15:8-12).

SON OF DAVID

Why would she have used this phrase, *"Son of David,"* when speaking to Christ?

Living as close as she did to Israel, she was probably well acquainted with the hopes and aspirations of the Jews respecting their coming Messiah.

Hearing the conversations of His great miracles and the discussion as to whether He was the Messiah, she, no doubt, concluded in her heart that Jesus was indeed the Messiah, the Son of David, in effect, the Son of God.

As a Gentile, she had no scriptural right to address Christ as the Son of David, but she probably did not know that. Her story is an example to all of us. Then again, maybe she thought that addressing Him as she did, this was the proper thing to do.

If the Lord demanded that our approach to Him be totally proper in every respect, most of us would fall by the wayside. Thankfully, He does not demand that. He only demands faith, and faith this woman had!

Even as I write these words, I strongly sense the presence of God. Even with tears, I feel the emotion of the moment as she approached Christ. I see myself in her, as you should as well.

She was out of dispensation, even unscriptural, and actually had no right to what she was asking; however, her petition would not be denied, and neither will the petition of anyone else be denied if we come in the manner in which she came—with humility and faith.

The Holy Spirit had this glorious example portrayed to us by both Matthew and Mark that its great lesson would not be lost upon us. If she received, you can receive as well! The pronoun *we* includes you.

MY DAUGHTER IS GRIEVOUSLY VEXED WITH A DEVIL (DEMON)

The woman now proclaimed to the Lord her dire need. It concerned her daughter. The child was demon possessed.

The Lord did not contradict her respecting the diagnosis, so, undoubtedly, demon powers were the cause of this affliction. This is a subject in which many are not knowledgeable. I speak of children being influenced or even possessed by demon spirits. Actually, this is not the exception, especially in the world in which she lived, or even in the world in which we live today.

Tragically, most children in America, or any country in the world for that matter, are raised in homes that little know God. They are subjected to profanity, immorality, and a very atmosphere that is charged by the powers of darkness.

Consequently, even as children, they provide a fertile territory for the activity of demon spirits.

If one could look into the spirit world, one would see demon spirits operating graphically so in the lives of many, if not most, teenagers and even preteens.

A DOCUMENTARY

In a documentary that I saw over television recently, the commentator was remarking about the callousness of some teenagers who had committed murder. "They seem to show no remorse whatsoever concerning the terrible thing they have done," she said. "Killing a fellow human being was no more to them than a flick of the wrist."

The ages of the two killers she interviewed were 12 and 14, if I remember correctly.

She was nonplussed over their attitudes, as well as the attitudes of multiple tens of thousands of other teenagers and preteens who exhibit traits that are completely unexplainable to the sociologists, psychologists, etc.

The answer now is the same as it was then: *"Vexed with a demon."*

There is only one answer to this terrible malady, and it, as well, is the same now as then—Jesus Christ and Him crucified. All of the sociologists and psychologists in the world cannot help such a one. This is the reason that the gospel preached in all of its power is so very important. It is the answer because it is the gospel of Christ.

A LETTER

Sometime back, we received a letter that explains what I am attempting to say. It was addressed to Frances:

Dear Mrs. Swaggart,

You probably wonder why I am writing this letter to you instead of your husband, but I feel this is a story that only a mother can understand. I know that you have a son, and I thought you might want to hear what God has done in my life.

I have always been privileged to stay home and take care of our only son. We live in a very exclusive neighborhood and have many of the luxuries not afforded to most.

Up until the past few years, I thought that nothing could touch the peace and prosperity of our world. Then one morning, 16 months ago, I awoke to find that our son, who was then 16, had left home in the middle of the night.

For about a year, we had fought an uphill battle with him. He had gotten into the wrong crowd—a gang-type group, whose leader seemed to have much more influence on him than my husband and I did. We have found marijuana in his room, pornographic literature, rock music—all the earmarks of teen-age trouble.

We immediately sought professional help for him, which we know now was definitely a mistake. We spent thousands of dollars, only to be told that we had failed in our efforts to raise our son, and that his rebellion was simply a natural response to our erroneous child rearing.

When he left, I have to admit to you that in one sense, I was relieved. I knew that we could not do any more for him, as the harder we tried, the more rebellious he became.

When our son was reported missing, we came to realize that he was on the long list of statistics. The police department made an earnest effort to locate him; but under the circumstances, we knew that he did not want to be found.

For a period of about six months, we did not hear from him at all. Then, we only heard through other teenagers who had once been his friends that he was living with this gang, and more or less living on the streets or in 'hop' houses, where sources of drugs were readily available. I don't think I have to tell you that I died a thousand deaths during this time.

Tuesday morning, three weeks ago, I answered the phone and realized that on the other end was my son. He said, 'Mom, I really need to talk to you. Something has happened to me. I am ready to come home.' Words cannot express to you just what went through my mind at that time. Tears ran like a river, and I was so happy, yet, I wondered, 'Is this real?' Would he come home only to repeat the scenario of the past? I don't think that his dad or I could stand that.

Late that afternoon, a prodigal son arrived on the doorsteps. He was dirty and bedraggled, his hair long and unkempt, and his arms scarred with needle tracks from shooting up. But, in spite of all this, there was a look in his eyes that was bright and happy, like I had not seen in two years.

After hugging and crying for what seemed like hours, he said, 'Mom, the strangest thing happened to me yesterday. I had gotten totally stoned the night before, had come in about daylight and crashed on the couch. I had been watching some sort of weird stuff on TV and went off to sleep. When I woke up, it was about 3:30 in the afternoon. On the channel where I had been watching, there was this preacher. Mom, it was the same one that I used to see Grandma watching when I was a kid. (My mother, until her death six years ago, always watched your program.) I thought about Grandma and how disappointed she would have been in me if she could see me now, and I started to cry. The preacher was talking about how no matter how bad you are, God still loves you and wants you to come home to Him. Then he prayed a prayer, and I said it with him. I said, 'God, I don't want to be like this. I don't want to shoot dope. I can't stop. Please help me.'

'This preacher's son was there with him praying. I wanted to be able to see my dad, and to have him be proud of me like this preacher is of his son. He talked about how his son was a preacher too. I thought about how I had disappointed Dad and you. I said, 'God, please forgive me for doing this to Mom and Dad. Please let them want me to come home.' Then I went to sleep again and didn't wake up until this morning. When I woke up, I knew that I had to come home, so I called you. Mom, this is the first time I haven't shot up in the morning for over a year, and I feel great.'

I was in a total state of shock! I wasn't even sure that I believed in miracles, but I had one standing here in front of my eyes. I have to admit that I was skeptical, and first of all, I had to know just who this preacher was that my son had seen. (He had not seen the program begin or end and did not know *the name.) I looked at the television listing at 3:30 p.m. on Monday on all the networks, and nothing was there except soaps. On most of the major cable stations we had children's programming and miscellaneous programs—nothing religious. I said, 'Do you know what station you were watching?' He said, 'Mom, all I know is that it is a station where they show atheist programs and stuff, and it was on a Monday afternoon.'*

The only thing I could think of that fit this description was People TV—the local public channel. Sure enough, when I looked on their listings, it said, 'Jimmy Swaggart.'

At 3:30 that next Monday, we turned on the program, and there was Jimmy Swaggart, singing and preaching. My son's eyes filled with tears, and he said, 'That's him, Mom, that's him.' We both wept and cried during the entire program.

My son is finally home. He is clean-shaven, has a haircut, and his clothes are clean. However, these are small, unimportant things. He has a new life. He has had no drugs or alcohol since he walked in my door again. We are looking for a good Bible-based church to attend.

Once again, let me thank you for being on People TV Channel 12. Thank God that Brother Swaggart has been able to withstand the attacks launched against him and is still preaching the gospel.

I have no idea just how your program happened to be aired on our little local channel, but please know that his father and I are so thankful to Brother Swaggart for helping us get our son back. Only the Lord will be able to relate to you just how your ministry has blessed this family!

This letter is just one of the many hundreds of thousands, or even millions, that we have received over the years telling of what Jesus Christ has done within a heart and a life. The only answer to these terrible problems is Christ and Him crucified.

THE MODERN CHURCH

Regrettably and sorrowfully, the modern church has become one great referral unit. It refers the alcoholic to Alcoholics Anonymous, the compulsive gambler to Gamblers Anonymous, etc.

As well, it refers those who are influenced or even possessed by demon spirits to the psychologists. To be sure and certain, there is little help from these sources.

Only Jesus can set the captive free.

Only Jesus can break the chains that bind humanity.

Only Jesus can save the lost soul.

Why are the churches, at least for the most part, doing this? They are doing it because most of them no longer preach the gospel or even believe the gospel. Most have denied, and are denying, the almighty power of the Holy Spirit. Consequently, there is no power in their services, their worship, or their preaching. As a result, no captives are set free. By and large, it is dead preachers preaching dead sermons to dead congregations.

However, I will say as Joshua of old, *"As for me and my house, we will serve the LORD"* (Josh. 24:15).

BUT HE ANSWERED HER NOT A WORD

"But He answered her not a word. And His disciples came and besought Him, saying, Send her away; for she crieth after us" (Mat. 15:23).

In the entirety of this scenario (as intended by the Holy Spirit), we are given a perfect description of how to approach the Lord and how to receive from the Lord. It will be an invaluable lesson.

His not addressing her or answering her was by design. Everything that Jesus did, even down to the words He spoke, was guided by the Holy Spirit. Therefore, as this scene unfolds before us, it is a carefully crafted plan engineered by the Holy Spirit in order to meet this woman's need, i.e., the healing and deliverance of her daughter.

So, His failure to answer was not meant at all to put her off or to deny her request, but instead, it was in order that she might receive what she had asked.

The ways of God are not our ways. However, His ways are meant for our good.

THE LESSON HERE TAUGHT

The lesson here taught and to be learned is that if the Lord does not answer immediately, we are not to stop our petition. The phrase, *"And cried unto Him,"* as given in the previous verse, meant that she kept crying. In other words, she would not stop.

It is regrettable that a great part of the church world is taught that we are only to ask the Lord one time and that any further petitions are a sign of a lack of faith. The Scripture abundantly proclaims that such is not true. If at first we do not receive, we are importuned to continue asking (Lk. 11:8).

As well, the delay, if there is delay, is not meant to be antagonizing to the seeker. The Lord does all things for a purpose. Along with giving us what we request, He, as well, always teaches us lessons by the manner in which He gives them. In other words, the lesson given and the manner in which it is given are all meant to serve as a teaching vehicle.

Regrettably, most Christians presently ask once or twice and then quickly tire, claiming that God does not answer prayer, or else, they give some other excuse.

The lesson taught in this experience is that if we do not at first receive, continue to ask and, as this woman of Canaan, continue asking in faith. Delay does not mean denial! It only means that we are to continue asking and believing.

AND HIS DISCIPLES CAME AND BESOUGHT HIM

The heading proclaims their doing this after her repeated petitions; however, if one is to notice, there is another potent truth in this phrase.

This woman of Canaan did not come to the disciples but to Jesus. It is sad when Catholicism erroneously encourages its people to pray to dead saints or even some of these disciples, or more particularly, Mary, the mother of Christ.

In the four gospels, which give the account of the ministry of the Master, one finds precious little evidence that individuals in need came to the disciples, but instead, directly to Christ. It would surely seem that the Holy Spirit is telling us something in these many accounts of seekers coming to Christ.

The truth is that all petitions must be made directly to the Father in the name of Jesus (Jn. 16:23). All other prayers and petitions are useless, with no help forthcoming whatsoever from these other sources because to do otherwise is unscriptural.

SAYING, SEND HER AWAY; FOR SHE CRIES AFTER US

The heading probably would have been better translated in another manner inasmuch as the true meaning is here obscured. It should have been translated, "Grant her request; for she cries after us." It seems they were perturbed because of her petition, and it was a loud petition at that. In other words, she would not stop her *"crying,"* and neither should we!

Every evidence is that the disciples grew impatient with her. To be frank, sadly, most of the hindrances of our present petitions come directly from the saints of God, even as the closest companions of Christ, His disciples. This is especially true if the answer is not forthcoming immediately. In other words, oftentimes, even the Lord's chosen children will discourage us; however, if we are asking in the will of God, we should not let anything deter us, even as this dear woman of Canaan did not let anything deter her.

This woman of Canaan suffered great trouble in the affliction of her daughter and was earnestly seeking help from Jesus. However, much more would be done for Christ if the church would cry to the Lord at this present time on behalf of individuals such as this woman of Canaan did.

BUT HE ANSWERED AND SAID

"But He answered and said, I am not sent but unto the lost sheep of the house of Israel" (Mat. 15:24).

The heading presents what seems to be another rebuke to the woman. Her faith would be sorely tested, which, no doubt, the Holy Spirit intended to do.

It should be well understood that this woman had absolutely nothing to offer the Lord except her faith, and even that was somewhat misplaced. Irrespective, it was faith, and it was faith in Christ, even as we shall see.

People all over the world are presenting things to God that are of no purpose and no use. He operates on one principle and one principle alone, and that is the principle of faith.

However, it must be faith in what Christ did for us at the Cross. Of course, this dear lady of so long ago knew nothing about a Cross and, in fact, neither did anyone else except the Lord. But now, ever since the Cross, the Cross of Christ is to ever be the object of our faith.

The Cross is that which makes everything possible. It opens the door to all the good things of God, in essence, the grace of God.

I AM NOT SENT BUT UNTO THE LOST
SHEEP OF THE HOUSE OF ISRAEL

The heading proclaims His mission, at least in His first advent, as exclusively to the Jews, although it would ultimately fall out to the entirety of the world (Jn. 3:16).

As a man, Christ was *"sent"* and was, therefore, a servant, hence, the silence of Matthew 15:23.

As God, He had liberty of action, and in grace, He could respond to the need that faith presented to that grace. Otherwise, He would have denied His own character and nature as God. He ultimately did respond to the need of the woman of Canaan.

Due to the prophecies and the plan of God, Jesus must first come to Israel. They were His people or, at least, should have been. All the great promises had been made to them; therefore, the gospel should be offered to them first before it was offered to the Gentiles, which it was.

THE PLAN OF GOD

Even from the very beginning, the plan of God was that Israel would accept their Messiah and then take His glorious message to the entirety of the world. This was God's intention from the very beginning as He told Abraham, *"In you shall all families of the earth be blessed"* (Gen. 12:3). However, the Jews refused to give that blessing to the Gentiles or even accept it themselves.

Respecting Israel, the words "*lost sheep*" are interesting indeed! Very few Jews, if any, would even think of admitting they were lost. However, they had by now come to the place that they believed simply being a Jew constituted their salvation. In other words, their salvation was their nationality, and their nationality was their salvation, or so they erroneously thought.

It is the same presently with most modern believers. Their association with a certain church is their salvation, and their salvation is their association with a certain church.

However, there is no salvation in nationality, as there is no salvation in association with any church.

UNCONDITIONAL ETERNAL SECURITY

The words "*lost sheep*" are interesting in another capacity as well. The modern teaching of unconditional eternal security claims that "once a sheep, always a sheep." However, Christ here says the very opposite. He calls Israel, or at least the greater part of it, "*lost sheep.*"

It meant that they were supposed to be His people, and in truth, some of them had once been His people. But now, these sheep had refused to recognize Christ as the Messiah or to accept Him as Saviour; therefore, in their refusal to do this, they did not discontinue being sheep but were, in fact, lost sheep.

As well, a modern believer, although at one time in faith, can cease to believe and then becomes what one might call a lost believer. These individuals were once in faith, and it certainly was God's will that they remain in faith, but by their own volition, they removed themselves. If they remain in that state, as Israel of old, they are lost.

As well, the word *lost* in the Greek is *apollumi* and means "to destroy fully; to perish." Consequently, it does not mean a loss merely of fellowship as some teach.

It is faith in Christ and what He did for us at the Cross that got us in, i.e., born again. If faith is maintained in Christ and the Cross, the individual is saved; however, if by one's own volition the person ceases to believe in Christ, he has removed himself from the grace of God.

A SINFUL LIFESTYLE

And then, there are some who truly come to Christ but want to maintain their sinful lifestyles. For instance, if a homosexual comes to Christ, the Lord will readily receive such a one as He will anyone; however, if that homosexual believes a lie and thinks that he or she can continue in that lifestyle and at the same time be saved, that person is mistaken. The Holy Spirit through the apostle Paul said the very opposite (Gal. 5:19-21). The same would go for any other type of sin listed in these passages.

Continuing to use the homosexual as an example, it is certainly true that such a person may accept the Lord and then have a struggle with this problem for a period of time after his or her salvation. In other words, he wants victory over this thing but finds it difficult to find that victory. That person is saved, even though he may fail the Lord at times by slipping back into his old lifestyle; however, it's not done purposely, and the truth is, he hates that lifestyle (or whatever kind of sin it might be) and is struggling, trying to quit. Ultimately, he will find victory if he perseveres.

THEN CAME SHE AND WORSHIPPED HIM

"Then came she and worshipped Him, saying, Lord, help me" (Mat. 15:25).

The heading seems to indicate (according to Mark) that Jesus had left the street where this woman of Canaan first approached Him and now went into a house, with her following. Once again, her persistence is greatly proclaimed. She had met two rebuffs already from Christ, or at least what probably seemed to her as such, but she was not deterred. Instead, she fell at His feet and worshipped Him. If one is to notice, she had graduated from petition to worship. To be sure, this entire episode is remarkable. The lessons contained therein should stand as a beacon of hope for all who believe God and are determined to receive certain things from Him.

SAYING, LORD, HELP ME

The phrase, *"Saying, Lord, help me,"* is actually a completely different petition than her first when she addressed Christ as *"Thou Son of David."* However, even though this plea, *"Lord, help me,"* was better than her first one, still, she did not get the blessing until she added, *"I am a dog."* This was the same ground the publican took when he said, *"Be merciful to me a sinner"* (Lk. 18:13).

FAITH

There are two things that dramatically stand out about this woman, which should be an example to us: First, she would not stop her petition. Second, she had a need, and she knew that Jesus was the only one who could meet that need. She was determined to get that for which she had come. We are constantly admonished in the Word of God to do the same (Mat. 21:21-22; Mk. 11:24; Lk. 11:8; Jn. 15:7).

However, we must understand that the object of our faith must ever be Jesus Christ and Him crucified (I Cor. 1:23). It is the Cross of Christ that opens up everything. Martin Luther said it, and he was right: "Unless one understands the Cross of Christ, one does not understand or have a correct knowledge of God." Now, as would be obvious, this woman would have no understanding of the Cross whatsoever, and neither did anyone else at that time other than Christ. However, according to the apostle Paul, since the Cross, our faith must ever be in Christ and what He did for us at the Cross (Rom. 6:3-5; 8:1-11; I Cor. 1:17-18, 23; 2:2; Gal. 6:14; Col. 2:10-15).

HUMILITY

This trait stands out so dramatically in the action of this lady. Despite the seeming rebuffs, she would fall at His feet and worship Him. How many believers presently hold a grudge against God because He did not do something they thought He should have done?

The truth is that none of us are worthy of anything from God, and until we understand that, the granted petitions are going to be few and far between.

Preachers are very fond of talking about one's rights in Christ. Despite teaching to the contrary, and even despite our having received the great born-again experience and becoming a child of God, still, we have no rights, only privileges. Jesus said, *"For whosoever exalteth himself shall be abased; and he who humbles himself shall be exalted"* (Lk. 14:11).

I wonder what the Lord must think of us demanding our rights. Far too often, healing, prosperity, and a host of other things are demanded as the rights of the believer. No! The only one who has rights is Christ. He alone is worthy *"to receive glory and honour and power"* (Rev. 4:11). All of these things, even being a joint heir with Christ, is but a privilege, but what a privilege it is!

BUT HE ANSWERED AND SAID

"But He answered and said, It is not meet to take the children's bread, and to cast it to dogs" (Mat. 15:26).

The heading will now constitute the third rebuff to this woman. It was a rebuff, at least as it looked outwardly, but in actuality, it was the manner in which she could receive that for which she came. What she was about to hear was going to be hard, but she knew what she wanted, and she was determined to get it.

Everything the Lord does with us is for an intended purpose. In other words, He is driving at something positive. He never chides us, never reprimands us, and never haughtily turns us away. If what He says seems to be harsh, as stated, it is for divine purpose. Most all of the time, it is our faith that needs attention. We may think that it is totally and completely sufficient, but actually, it isn't. So, the Lord will answer this woman in a way that may seem harsh, but at the same time, it will garner the intended results.

IT IS NOT MEET TO TAKE THE CHILDREN'S BREAD, AND TO CAST IT TO DOGS

The statement is strong indeed! In effect, He was calling her a dog, which she readily understood. As well, this word *dog* meant the lowest form of the canine variety—a cur dog.

So, in effect, He was speaking of her and her people as being idol worshipers and, in fact, some of the worst kind. As stated, they were worshipers of Baal and Ashtaroth, which signaled the worst form of depravity and pollution.

"Children's bread" referred to Israel, who were recipients of the promises and the prophets and, in effect, were the only ones in the world who had any knowledge of Jehovah. Consequently, they are called children, i.e., God's children, at least those who actually were, which were few. The word *bread* speaks of the Word of God and all that it entails.

In truth, Jesus' own people, the Jews, were in worse spiritual condition even than these heathen. They were worse simply because they had been given the light, albeit rejected, while the Gentiles had been given precious little light at all. That is the reason Jesus placed a curse upon Israel, and He used the very area from which this woman came as an example by saying, *"For if the mighty works, which were done in you* (Israel), *had been done in Tyre and Sidon, they would have repented long ago in sackcloth and ashes"* (Mat. 11:21). So, if these—Tyre and Sidon—were *"dogs,"* what category must Israel fall into?

AND SHE SAID, TRUTH, LORD

"And she said, Truth, Lord: yet the dogs eat of the crumbs which fall from their masters' table" (Mat. 15:27). The heading proclaims her acknowledging her position as undeserving and without legal covenant rights to the children's bread.

This woman suffered three rebuffs:

1. *"He answered her not a word."* This concerns her first petition when she spoke of her daughter.
2. *"I am not sent but unto the lost sheep of the house of Israel* (My mission is only to Israel)*."* This, in fact, excluded her, but she responded by worshipping Him.
3. *"It is not meet to take the children's bread, and to cast it to dogs* (He called her a dog, which was the worst cut of all)*."* By this time, most would have left, but not her. In fact, the answer that she gave Him is one of the greatest answers of faith in recorded history.

In all of this, this woman was saying that she had no claim on the Lord. She realized that she was but a heathen, a Gentile dog. All of this was true, and she admitted to it.

What made this woman persist in her petition?

PERSISTENCE

Of course, the ready answer would be that her daughter was in a terrible condition and desperately needed help. While all of that is true, still, there must have been something about Christ, despite His response to her, that caused her to press on until the victory came.

To be sure, there was something about Christ—even though His statements to her were negative, even extremely so, still, His entire manner and personality were of pure love. This must have encouraged her to press forward.

This should be a lesson to us that even though the situation may be critical, with even our wrong or sin most terrible, which demands judgment, still, to any and all who come to Him, they will find Him always to be loving, kind, considerate, compassionate, longsuffering, and quick to forgive.

YET THE DOGS EAT OF THE CRUMBS WHICH FALL FROM THEIR MASTERS' TABLE

The answer this woman gave turned the words of Christ back to Himself. She used His own words as a means in which to receive healing and deliverance for her daughter. This in no way would abrogate His mission to Israel, but at the same time, would grant her request. She, in effect, was saying, "The Jews are the children, while we are the dogs, but, as dogs, we claim our portion, even if only crumbs."

One can sense the presence of the Lord even in the saying of these words. This lady is an example to us all, as the Holy Spirit intended her to be.

Most believers (and I do not believe that I exaggerate) try to find ways as to why God will not do certain things. To be sure, that list is endless; however, this dear lady did the very opposite. She turned every negative into a positive, every darkness into a light, and every no into a yes! What she was doing was totally scriptural. Paul would later say, *"For all the promises of God in Him are yes, and in Him Amen, unto the glory of God by us"* (II Cor. 1:20).

"Then Jesus answered and said unto her, O woman, great is your faith: be it unto you even as you will. And her daughter was made whole from that very hour" (Mat. 15:28).

THEN JESUS ANSWERED AND SAID UNTO HER ...

The heading is emphasized by the word *then.*

All of the time, the Holy Spirit had been drawing her to this place, and now she would receive that for which she had come.

Did Jesus change His mind?

No! He wanted her to have her petition all along, but He had to bring her to the place to where she could receive it. It was true that these other situations were hurdles that had to be overcome; however, faith can overcome any and every hurdle, as Jesus now proclaimed.

The moral of the story and the lesson the Holy Spirit is teaching is the lesson of faith. As well, it is the type of faith that will not be denied.

O WOMAN, GREAT IS YOUR FAITH

The heading proclaims His answer to her persistence. As well, what she had was *"great faith."* Only two people are spoken of as having great faith. The first was the Gentile centurion who came for the healing of his servant (Mat. 8:5-10), and now this Gentile woman. What a rebuke to Israel!

BE IT UNTO YOU EVEN AS YOU WILL

The heading proclaims, as is obvious, her getting exactly what she wanted. What a lesson for all others!

While it is true that the Lord will definitely give to the believing saints that which we want or desire, still, what we want or desire must be in line with what the Holy Spirit wants as well! The following may seem negative; however, I feel that in light of the times, what will be said is necessary.

ERRONEOUS DIRECTION

Since the 1970s, this idea of getting what we want has been taken to excess. Scores of believers, thinking they automatically know the will of God in all things, have begun to ask for all types of things, even foolish things, which shows a terrible spiritual immaturity. If believers sincerely and truly want the will of God in their lives and are constantly seeking that will, they will, as well, pray in the will of God. If the Holy Spirit is helping us pray, which He certainly will, at least if we are striving constantly for God's will, we will never pray for anything that is not desired for us by the heavenly Father (Rom. 8:26-27).

Many have taken various Scriptures in the Word of God, such as Matthew 21:21-22; Mark 11:24; John 14:14; 15:7, etc., and have attempted to apply these passages to any and all things, claiming that they portray the will of God in these matters. As well, they say that if we do not receive whatever we want (whatever that is), it shows a lack of faith on our part. Such is not a lack of faith, but rather is presumption!

While it is certainly true that the Word of God means exactly what it says, still, these promises are meant to carry out His will and not our will. Even in Scriptures such as Mark 11:24, our will is supposed to be His will, and we are to desire nothing that He does not desire. If we sincerely want the will of God, that is exactly what we will get—His will!

USING THE WORD OF GOD AGAINST GOD

The most dangerous thing a Christian can do is to attempt to use the Word of God against God, which refers to trying to force the situation, whatever it might be.

It is perfectly permissible, and even encouraged, for us to take God's Word and apply it to our situations exactly as this woman of Canaan did. Still, it must be in the will of God exactly as the deliverance of this woman's daughter was.

Of course, the will of God is the Word of God; however, He will not allow His Word to be used against Himself.

As an example, all of these faith Scriptures we have just noted could definitely apply to the acquiring of great wealth. In fact, the major thrust of a large segment of the charismatic community has been exactly this—to acquire riches. However, what does the Bible say? Paul said:

> But godliness with contentment is great gain. For we brought nothing into this world, and it is certain we can carry nothing out. And having food and raiment let us be therewith content. But they who will be rich fall into temptation and a snare, and into many foolish and hurtful lusts, which drown men in destruction and perdition. For the love of money is the root of all evil: which while some coveted after, they have erred from the faith, and pierced themselves through with many sorrows. But you, O man of God, flee these things; and follow after righteousness, godliness, faith, love, patience, meekness (I Tim. 6:6-11).

THE BLESSING

And yet, God richly blesses His people also in the financial sense. In fact, believers who are striving to walk in the will of God should expect God to bless them. That's not wrong, with encouragement from the Word of God tendered toward such; however, if God does bless economically and financially, we should care for our family and then use the balance to further His work all over the world.

The making of money is not to be the primary factor in our lives, but rather carrying out the will of God, whatever that will might be. I am convinced that God would grandly bless more Christians economically if they could be trusted. However, I am concerned that most cannot be trusted.

In my years of evangelistic work, preaching the gospel all over the world, which has taken large sums of money, I have watched the Lord bless some people, with it seemingly hurting them instead of helping them. I have noted a few who have been blessed by the Lord abundantly so, and who in turn blessed His work greatly. Regrettably, that number is few.

JESUS, THE EPITOME OF THE WILL OF GOD

In truth, Jesus was the epitome of the will of God. His actions as well as His message portrayed God's will in every capacity. Everything He did was totally in the will of God, meaning that He constantly sought that perfect will. In this, several things become obvious.

He healed everyone who came to Him, irrespective of their spiritual condition. Therefore, from this example, we must assume that it is always God's will to heal the sick. However, all of us know that oftentimes, even good Christians fail to receive healing even though they earnestly petition the Lord. Even Paul said, *"But Trophimus have I left at Miletum sick"* (II Tim. 4:20).

I think all would have to assume that Paul had great faith, even with many great miracles performed in his ministry. Still, at times individuals were not healed, as is here recorded.

Of course, the question must be asked, "If it is always the will of God to heal the sick, even as Christ portrayed, why aren't they always healed?" I suppose that question has been asked by every faith-filled believer since the time of Christ.

THE LORD JESUS CHRIST

I personally believe that the only answer (which I have already commented on) is that no believer can come up to the status of Christ in his faith or life. While it is true that all sincere believers truly strive to be like Christ, still, at the same time, all of us fall woefully short (Rom. 3:23).

As well, the manner in which Jesus conducted His ministry portrayed the coming kingdom age. It was offered to Israel, but they rejected it. But yet, Christ continued to conduct His ministry in that fashion. In other words, when the kingdom age comes, which will commence at the second coming, the greatest worldwide healing meetings the world has ever known are going to take place. This will present not only our Lord healing all the sick but, as well, the glorified saints doing the same thing. During that time, sickness is going to be a thing of the past. That means that during that time, there will be no need for doctors, hospitals, nurses, etc.

In fact, the leaves that grow on the trees that border the river that comes out from under the threshold in the temple in Jerusalem will be for healing. This refers to multiple thousands, even tens of thousands, of trees. Actually, *"the leaf thereof for medicine"* will be more so in the preventive capacity than anything else (Ezek. 47:12). Of course, this will be for the natural people on earth at that time and not for the glorified saints, for they will need nothing in that capacity. So, to use the ministry of Christ while He was on earth as an example is only permissible up to a point. As stated, He was then functioning in the realm of the kingdom age, but we know that because of Israel's rejection, that age has not yet arrived. So, Israel's rejection of Christ submitted the world to a further 2,000 years of sorrow and heartache. That will end at the second coming.

INTERCESSION

Along with all the other valuable lessons taught us in the portrayal as it regards this woman of Canaan, the tremendous lesson of intercession on behalf of another, as this mother, should not be lost upon us. To be sure, most, if not all, who come to the Lord do so simply because someone, as this woman, interceded before the Lord for them.

Regrettably, most of the energy of the church in the last few years has been spent on trying to get rich instead of this all-important task. Satan has successfully appealed to the covetousness in the hearts and lives of many and successfully drawn them away from that which is all-important—the salvation of souls.

"And Jesus departed from thence, and came near unto the Sea of Galilee; and went up into a mountain, and sat down there" (Mat. 15:29).

AND JESUS DEPARTED FROM THENCE

The heading refers to Christ leaving the border of Israel and going to the east side of the Sea of Galilee. We learn from Mark that Jesus came to the cities of Decapolis, which were located on the eastern side.

AND CAME NEAR UNTO THE SEA OF GALILEE

The heading refers to a hill near this body of water. It was probably near Bethsaida.

As we have previously stated, the Sea of Galilee is about 14 miles long and some seven miles wide. It is a beautiful body of water, which the Holy Spirit chose to serve basically as the headquarters of our Lord in His earthly sojourn of ministry.

AND WENT UP INTO A MOUNTAIN, AND SAT DOWN THERE

The heading indicates that Jesus had evidently come at other times to this place to rest; however, such at this time was not to be, even as we shall see.

"And great multitudes came unto Him, having with them those who were lame, blind, dumb, maimed, and many others, and cast them down at Jesus' feet; and He healed them" (Mat. 15:30).

AND GREAT MULTITUDES CAME UNTO HIM

The great multitudes could well have represented several thousand people. This was to be the greatest day of their lives. As well, it is by far the high point for any and all who come to Jesus. There is no life like a life lived for Him. There is no joy like that with which He fills the soul.

Incidentally, it will be this way in the coming kingdom age, but multiplied many times over. In other words, people will be coming from all over the world at that time, seeking healing, seeking information, and seeking knowledge, and they will not leave disappointed. Of that, one can be certain.

Scientists will come from all over the world seeking the information that only Christ can give as it regards particulars of whatever nature. Those who are interested in growing crops will come to Jerusalem to seek the leading and the guidance of the Lord as it regards farming, and again, they will not leave disappointed. In fact, every type of knowledge that one can think will be dispensed from Jerusalem, and, of course, we speak of Christ. As I dictate these notes, the religious leader of Iran recently made the statement that in 25 years Israel will not even be in existence.

Well, the truth is according to the following: In fact, in the coming kingdom age when the Lord Jesus Christ will rule the entirety of the world as King of kings and Lord of lords, Israel will be the leading nation of the world. Actually, she will be the priestly nation one might say. As it regards Iran (Persia), it will be no more, forever to cease as a nation. So, regarding what the Iranian leader said, the very opposite is going to take place.

HAVING WITH THEM THOSE WHO WERE LAME, BLIND, DUMB, MAIMED, AND MANY OTHERS

The heading proclaims about every type of physical malady known to man. As well, what is said physically can also be said spiritually for any and all! It is interesting that the word *maimed* is used in that it means "one who is crippled," but it also means "one who has been deprived of a limb," such as the loss of an arm, a leg, etc. There is no passage in the four gospels that specifically states that Jesus replaced missing limbs, with the exception of the servant's ear that was cut off by Simon Peter in the garden of Gethsemane (Lk. 22:50-51; Jn. 18:10). In this incident, Jesus, no doubt, had the severed ear replaced on the servant's head where He healed it. However, He could easily have replaced missing limbs even though they had long since been gone, for such was certainly within the realm of His power.

AND CAST THEM DOWN AT JESUS' FEET ...

The heading denotes scores, possibly many hundreds, attempting to get to Christ and even throwing themselves at His feet. For many of them, their situation was desperate; therefore, they used desperate measures.

AND HE HEALED THEM

The heading implies that He healed them all.

There is no record in the Word of God of anyone who came to Christ being turned away. Neither does He turn anyone away today and, in fact, never has and never will.

"Insomuch that the multitude wondered, when they saw the dumb to speak, the maimed to be whole, the lame to walk, and the blind to see: and they glorified the God of Israel" (Mat. 15:31).

INSOMUCH THAT THE MULTITUDE WONDERED

The heading means that they were stricken with astonishment when they saw the tremendous miracles. The attitude was one of tremendous joy coupled with astonishment at what was happening before their very eyes. Actually, neither they nor anyone else for that matter had ever seen anything like this. It made no difference what type of illness it was, how deformed the person was, or even how near death, Jesus healed them all. This is the way that it's going to be in the coming kingdom age. As the multitude wondered then, the multitude will wonder now.

WHEN THEY SAW

This short phrase means that they looked intently on what was happening. Before their very eyes, they watched the blind be led to Him, and then in a moment's time, the man or woman formerly blind was shouting, "I can see, I can see!"

As well, the cripples were led to Him, and then in a moment's time, the crippled leg was made every whit whole right before the eyes of all who stood nearby. No doubt, there was every type of miracle performed that could be imagined.

THE DUMB TO SPEAK, THE MAIMED TO BE WHOLE, THE LAME TO WALK, AND THE BLIND TO SEE

Inasmuch as the Holy Spirit through Matthew used the word *lame,* signifying those who are crippled, along with the word *maimed,* which, as we have stated, could signify a missing limb, finger, etc., this could mean that missing limbs were instantly replaced. This, no doubt, happened, and happened before the very eyes of the onlookers.

Let us say it again: There was no disease, no matter how bad it was, that He could not heal. There is no biblical record whatsoever that He failed in even one instance, even to the raising of the dead. What a mighty God we serve!

AND THEY GLORIFIED THE GOD OF ISRAEL

The heading proclaims the wave of glory and blessing that must have swept through that crowd. The power of God must have been so real at this time that every single individual witnessed and experienced it. Truly, heaven had come down to earth!

The implication is that they were not only glorifying God for the tremendous miracles performed but, as well, for the tremendous moving of the Holy Spirit that took place in their midst through the ministry of Christ.

There had never been another day like this in human history, except for the other times when Jesus did accordingly.

And yet, the religious leaders of Israel did not at all glorify God at these wonderful happenings but, instead, accused Christ of working in league with Satan (Mat. 12:24). There is no darkness like religious darkness!

THE SECOND COMING OF CHRIST

This which mankind experienced that glorious day of so long ago will once again be experienced at the second coming of Christ. Then the multitudes will come to Him exactly as they did at His first advent, and once again, this scene will repeat itself, except it will be on a worldwide basis. Then, thankfully, Israel will not reject Christ but will accept Him. The world will then know a time of blessing and prosperity such as it has never known before in all of its history.

As the multitude that day glorified the God of Israel, then the entirety of the world will glorify the God of Israel.

All the way my Saviour leads me,
What have I to ask beside?
Can I doubt His tender mercy,
Who through life has been my Guide?
Heavenly peace, divinest comfort,
Here by faith in Him to dwell;
For I know whate'er befall me,
Jesus doeth all things well,
For I know whatever befalls me,
Jesus does all things well."

All the way my Saviour leads me,
Cheers each winding path I tread;
Gives me grace for every trial,
Feeds me with the living bread.
Though my weary steps may falter,
And my soul athirst may be,
Gushing from the rock before me,
Lo! A spring of joy I see.
Gushing from the rock before me,
Lo! A spring of joy I see.

All the way my Saviour leads me,
O, the fullness of His love;
Perfect rest to me is promised,
In my Father's house above.

When my spirit, clothed immortal,
Wings its flight to realms of day,
This, my song through endless ages,
Jesus led me all the way,
This my song through endless ages,
Jesus led me all the way.

DIVINE *Healing*

CHAPTER 6

PRAYER

PRAYER

"IS ANY AMONG YOU afflicted? let him pray. Is any merry? let him sing psalms" (James 5:13).

IS ANY AMONG YOU AFFLICTED? LET HIM PRAY

The heading refers to trouble of any kind. Actually, just how valuable is prayer?

Considering that the Holy Spirit had told James what to say here as it regards affliction and prayer, the child of God should readily know and understand just how valuable and important that a proper prayer life actually is.

Every one of us would agree, that is, if we are saved, that Jesus Christ was and is perfect. Above that, He was and is the Son of God. As well, He was possessed by the Holy Spirit as no other human being has ever been possessed of this nature and in this capacity. And yet, He had an extremely strong prayer life. So, the question could be asked, If Jesus had to pray, how do we think we can eliminate this all-important principle and privilege?

One could probably say without any fear of scriptural exaggeration that prayer is the greatest privilege afforded the child of God. Without a proper prayer life, it is impossible for one to have a relationship with Christ. In fact, one of the great works carried out in our lives by the Holy Spirit is to help us pray (Rom. 8:26). And yet, so few Christians take advantage of this tremendous opportunity. Why?

WHY?

Satan fights the prayer life of a Christian as he fights nothing else. If he can defeat you on this front, he can defeat you on every front; and conversely, if he cannot defeat you on this front, he can little defeat you on any other front.

Unbelief is the culprit in many hearts and lives. Christians just simply do not believe that God answers prayer. One of the favorite statements is, "I've tried it, and it doesn't do anything for me," or words to that effect.

Trying prayer is like trying the Cross. Both statements are foolish. It's like saying, "I've tried breathing."

Of course, I'm certain that the reader understands that when we speak of prayer, even as James proclaims here, we are not speaking of such as a ritual or a ceremony, but rather communication and fellowship with the Lord. It is possible to turn prayer into works, but considering how few Christians actually pray, I think that such does not present very much of a problem.

PETITIONS AND PRAISES

Of the entirety of my life and living for the Lord, most all of the direction that I've ever received from the Holy Spirit has been while in prayer. I personally believe that we should take every single problem to the Lord, no matter how large or small it might be. We should ardently seek His leading and guidance in all things, once again, whether little or large. Most of all, most of our praying should be taken up with praise to the Lord, especially considering His great goodness to us, which comes in an uninterrupted flow. Our petitions should be small in number while our praises should be many.

Unfortunately, many in the modern church have eliminated prayer from their vocabulary, and even their thinking I suppose, in favor of counseling, when, in reality, the greatest Counselor of all lives within our hearts. Of course, I'm speaking of the Holy Spirit. How so foolish to ignore this tremendous privilege, and rather solicit the counsel of weak men.

PRAYER AND THE CROSS

As with everything else that pertains to the Word of God, I personally feel that our prayer lives can be greatly enhanced if we have a proper understanding of the Cross of Christ. In fact, I know it can. To have such an understanding helps us to comprehend the means by which the grace of God comes to us, which all of us must have on a continued basis. It is the Cross that makes grace possible, plus everything else that comes to us from the Lord. Without exception, every single prayer that's ever been uttered by a man to God, and every answer that God has ever given as it regards prayer, has always come through the means of the finished work of Christ. In fact, were it not for the Cross, the Lord could not even look at us, much less help us as He now can presently do. By and through that sacrifice alone can God deal with sinful man. So, if we understand that (I cannot really see how it is that we cannot), then we surely should understand how important such comprehension actually is, especially as it pertains to prayer.

WHY THE CROSS?

If we do not understand the Cross as the means by which God deals with man and man with God, then we will try to approach God on an entirely wrong basis. I speak of the basis of good works, merit, religion, etc. It should be readily understood that such an approach could never be accepted by the Lord.

In fact, every single praise that we as Christians might utter, such as "thank You, Jesus" or "praise the Lord," can be accepted by the Lord only on the basis of the slain Lamb, i.e., *"the Lamb of God"* (Jn. 1:29). Without the Cross, the door is irrevocably closed!

Some may wonder as to the validity of the position of believers before the Cross.

In a sense, the access by believers before the Cross was actually the same as it is now—faith in the one who was coming, which was represented by the sacrifices. Of course, access was to a far greater degree much more limited then than now, but the point is that the Cross has always been the means by which God has dealt with man and man with God. The sacrifices that were instituted immediately after the fall were the symbol of that which was to come. Even though the blood of bulls and goats couldn't take away sin, still, such sacrifices served as a means of faith. In other words, the offerer was to have faith in who they represented, and more particularly, what they represented. Of course, they represented Christ and the Cross. At the Cross Jesus atoned for all sin—past, present, and future, at least for all those who will believe (Jn. 3:16). With all sin removed, this makes it possible for God to deal with the human race on an entirely different level. That's why we say the Cross opens the door for everything, and without the Cross, there is no open door so to speak.

Martin Luther said, and I'm paraphrasing, If one doesn't understand the Cross as one should, this means that one has a very limited knowledge as to Who God actually is. In other words, one can only know God by and through the Cross of Christ.

The problem with the modern church is that it has a modicum of understanding respecting the Cross of Christ regarding salvation, but no understanding at all as it regards the great part the Cross plays in sanctification. In fact, 99 percent of Paul's writings have to do with the Cross of Christ as it pertains to our sanctification (our holiness), in other words, how we live for God on a daily basis. If the Holy Spirit devoted that much time and attention to this all-important subject, we should start to realize how important it really is. As previously stated, when we consider that the modern church understands almost nothing about the Cross as it regards our sanctification, then we should realize the reason for the present spiritual condition of the modern church.

IS ANY MERRY? LET HIM SING PSALMS

The heading, in effect, refers to singing as a form of prayer and of worship, which it actually is, that is, if we sing the right songs.

The *"psalms,"* of course, had to do with the book of Psalms that we have in our Bible, which was actually the only songbook that the church had at that particular time. There is a record of Christians in the early church beginning to compose particular songs based on scriptural doctrine, and even based on the psalms, but the psalms, at least in those days, provided the base and foundation for this tremendous form of worship.

To understand just how important this worship actually is, or at least the significance that God places upon this act, we should understand that the book of Psalms is the largest book in the Bible, and that's not without design. Consequently, we have the ideal combination of prayer and worship.

I think the Holy Spirit is telling us that if there would be more singing of psalms and spiritual songs, there would be less trouble.

This is so important that as much as Satan fights prayer, he, as well, opposes proper, scriptural worship and praise.

He does so through the music; I speak of that which goes under the name of Christian contemporary music, which means that it's very similar to that of the world. Such is not of God! I know that's blunt, but it is the truth. So, if it's not of God, that means that it's actually of Satan.

My grandson, Gabriel, was telling me a short time ago how that many of the so-called Christian rock groups, or whatever they call themselves, actually state that they get their inspiration from the most notorious groups in the nation, and the world for that matter. They are proclaiming blasphemy every time they open their mouths. Now, please tell me, how in the world can anything be of God when its inspiration is the Devil? Seemingly, they are proud of their association with these demonic groups and are quick to say so on their CDs as it regards the notes concerning the songs. Such music is of Satan. It's not just merely wrong, it is instigated by demon spirits, and it has invaded the church pell-mell.

Although some poor, misguided souls may claim to try to worship the Lord with such nonsense, the truth is that it is impossible to worship the Lord in any capacity by and of such music. In the creation of music, one might say that the Lord designed it as a trinity of melody, rhythm, and harmony. If any one of these three is perverted, it becomes impossible to worship. To make a bad matter worse, contemporary music corrupts both the melody and the harmony.

Such music made its debut in the 1960s as a copy of the music of the world. It was begun under the guise of reaching the youth but has degenerated presently to the mere spectacle of making money. To be sure, while it reached the youth, it reached them for Satan and not the Lord.

If Satan can pervert the music of the church, he has destroyed the church. Regrettably, he has perverted the music of the modern church.

"Is any sick among you? let him call for the elders of the church; and let them pray over him, anointing him with oil in the name of the Lord" (James 5:14).

IS ANY SICK AMONG YOU?

The question refers to physical illness of any nature. Let me say immediately that I thank God for doctors, nurses, hospitals, and for modern medicine. I feel that these things are a blessing of the Lord. In fact, I think we Christians should pray constantly that God will give medical scientists the knowledge to find the cure for certain diseases such as cancer. No, the Lord doesn't need help from anyone, but He does use doctors and nurses, as He uses many things.

Divine healing refers to being healed by the Lord as a result of believing prayer. As James proclaims here, physical sickness with divine healing is a major topic in the thinking of many Christians, even as it should be. However, many questions arise, including:

- Is it always God's will to heal the sick?
- Is all healing predicated totally and solely on the degree of faith that one might have in the Lord?
- Does God at times use sickness as a form of chastisement?

- Can some sicknesses be caused by demon spirits?
- Does the taking of medicine weaken or hinder our faith?
- Is healing in the atonement?

These questions and many others need to be biblically addressed. Unfortunately, many Christians are taught things that aren't exactly scriptural, and such teaching always brings forth bitter fruit. In other words, to the degree that we misinterpret the Word of God in any respect, to that degree we will suffer some loss. The Scripture tells us that the Holy Spirit *"will guide you into all truth"* (Jn. 16:13). While it is certainly true that no believer (preachers included) has all the light on any subject in the Word of God, still, we are definitely required by the Lord to walk in all the light that we presently have. So, every believer should *"study to show yourself approved unto God, a workman that needs not to be ashamed, rightly dividing the word of truth"* (II Tim. 2:15).

Let's look at what the Word of God says about physical healing.

SICKNESS AND HEALTH

A certain woman's only son was sick (I Ki. 17:7-24).

And it came to pass after these things, that the son of the woman, the mistress of the house, fell sick; and his sickness was so sore, that there was no breath left in him" (I Ki. 17:17). In frustration the woman turned to her boarder, the prophet Elijah, and cried out, *"What have I to do with you, O you man of God? are you come unto me to call my sin to remembrance, and to kill my son?"* (I Ki. 17:18).

Her reaction is not unusual. Many view sickness as punishment for sin, and there is a basis in the Bible for that view, at least in some cases. However, can all sickness be so directly linked with God's response to human behavior? Perhaps more significantly, can believers who walk closely with the Lord expect health and healing at all times? Let us look into some of these questions.

THE HEBREW WORDS

The Old Testament vocabulary of sickness includes terms for disease, for ailments, and for weakness or illness. However, the root word from which most of these are derived is *halah,* which means "to be weak or sick."

The concept includes weakness caused by illness (I Ki. 14:1; II Ki. 20:1, 12) and by wounds suffered in some way (II Chron. 18:33). At times the concept of weakness is extended as a metaphor of national weakness regarding the entirety of a nation (Hos. 5:13-14).

Sickness can also be a matter of the heart and portray mental and spiritual anguish (Ps. 38:5; Prov. 13:12; Song of Sol. 2:5). And yet, considering the span of time and subjects the Old Testament covers, it has surprisingly few references to illness or sickness in general. Even more surprising, in a language that often multiplies metaphors, sickness and disease are seldom used as symbols of something else.

The Hebrew word for health is also limited. It is *rapa* and means "to heal" or "to make healthy." It stands in contrast to the vocabulary of sickness. In contrast to weakness, there is strength; in contrast to debilitating illness, there is health and wholeness.

THE COVENANT OF HEALING

Almost immediately after delivering the children of Israel from Egyptian bondage, actually, after they had gone only a short distance into the wilderness, the Scripture says, *"And they went three days in the wilderness, and found no water"* (Ex. 15:22).

When they finally did find water, they found the water to be bitter, therefore, unusable. The Scripture tells us that Moses *"cried unto the* LORD*."* It then says:

"And the LORD *showed him a tree, which when he had cast into the waters, the waters were made sweet: there He made for them a statute and an ordinance, and there He proved them"* (Ex. 15:25).

At this time the great covenant of healing was given to Israel. It says: *"If you will diligently hearken to the voice of the* LORD *your God, and will do that which is right in His sight, and will give ear to His commandments, and keep all His statutes, I will put none of these diseases upon you, which I have brought upon the Egyptians: for I am the* LORD *who heals you"* (Ex. 15:26).

A TYPE OF THE CROSS

Of course, we know and realize that the *"tree"* was a type of the Cross, which alone could and can make sweet the bitter waters of life.

I personally think that the reason sickness and healing are not mentioned that much in the Old Testament is because of this great covenant of healing that Israel had with the Lord. But yet, we know and realize that Israel did not do too very well in giving ear to God's commandments or keeping all His statutes. So, there definitely was some sickness, etc., but I personally think that because of this covenant, the health of the Israelites was far ahead of the people of surrounding nations.

THE COVENANT OF HEALING PRESENTLY

As well, I might quickly add the following: Even though this covenant was made with Israel of old, at the same time, we know that the Word of God is immutable (not capable of or susceptible to change). In fact, we have the promise of even more under the new covenant than they had under the old (Heb. 8:6). Paul wrote:

> *But now* (since the Cross) *has He* (the Lord Jesus) *obtained a more excellent ministry* (the new covenant in Jesus' blood is superior and takes the place of the old covenant in animal blood), *by how much also He is the mediator of a better covenant* (proclaims the fact that Christ officiates between God and man according to the arrangements of the new covenant), *which was established upon better promises.* (This presents the new covenant, explicitly based on the cleansing and forgiveness of all sin, which the old covenant could not do) (Heb. 8:6) (The Expositor's Study Bible).

SICKNESS AND GOD

The Old Testament unquestionably relates sickness to God. In the Old Testament, in fact, all things are oriented to the Lord as their ultimate cause. Moses promised Israel, *"And you shall serve the LORD your God, and He shall bless your bread, and your water; and I will take sickness away from the midst of you"* (Ex. 23:25).

Likewise, disobedience to God would be punished at times by sickness. If Israel refused to obey the law and to revere God, there was this dreadful warning: *"Moreover He will bring upon you all the diseases of Egypt, which you were afraid of; and they shall cleave unto you. Also every sickness, and every plague, which is not written in the book of this law, them will the LORD bring upon you, until you be destroyed"* (Deut. 28:60-61).

Solomon's prayer at the dedication of the temple shows the same close relationship between God and illness. He said:

> *If there be dearth in the land, if there be pestilence, if there be blasting, or mildew, locusts, or caterpillars; if their enemies besiege them in the cities of their land; whatsoever sore or whatsoever sickness there be: Then what prayer or what supplication soever shall be made of any man, or of all Your people Israel, when everyone shall know his own sore and his own grief, and shall spread forth his hands in this house: Then hear you from heaven Your dwelling place, and forgive, and render unto every man according unto all his ways, whose heart You know; (for You only know the hearts of the children of men [Israel]) (II Chron. 6:28-30).*

However, even though sickness may strike the land or an individual as a direct act of God, it is not always so. Sickness is a reality that affects all of humanity, and we might quickly add that it is because of the fall. Also, even a prophet could develop a terminal illness (II Ki. 13:14).

SICKNESS AND SIN

Even though sickness is not always caused by sin, still, the link between the two can be seen throughout the Old Testament. One can note the Mosaic law's clear promise to Israel of divine protection from disease if they were obedient and its warning of illness if they were disobedient.

The link continues to shape the view of later Old Testament writers and is expressed in a number of ways. Psalms 103:3 parallels forgiveness and sin, healing and sickness. It is the Lord who forgives all your sins and heals all your diseases. Isaiah portrays sinful Israel as severely injured by blows from the Lord but unwilling still to turn to Him (Isa. 1:5-6).

Hosea speaks of national weakness as illness—illness that has come because of unconfessed sin. Until Israel admitted guilt and earnestly sought the Lord, there would be no rescue (Hos. 5:13-14).

These passages shoot down the unscriptural doctrine of the so-called grace revolution, which is no revolution at all. This false message teaches that when Christians sin, they should not confess that sin to the Lord and, in fact, should ignore it. Let us say this quickly: Unconfessed sin is unforgiven sin, and such a path will lead to terrible difficulties if not remedied.

The great prophet Hosea also said, *"Come, and let us return unto the LORD: for He has torn, and He will heal us; He has smitten, and He will bind us up"* (Hos. 6:1).

We find here that healing is found, therefore, in a return to the Lord. He who caused the injury is able to restore.

IS ALL SICKNESS CAUSED BY SIN?

No! All sickness is not a result of sin. Sickness comes at times, and even comes to all, as a natural consequence of human frailty, which, as stated, is a result of the fall.

And yet, whatever the nature or cause of sickness, it is appropriate to look to God for help, ever how He will bring about that help. Prayer and fasting are fitting, and when prayer for healing goes unanswered, the humbling of the soul is proper (Ps. 35:13-14).

Sickness, like all suffering and tragedy, cannot automatically be assigned to sin or ascribed to God's judgment on a sinner. It certainly may be that at times, but it definitely is not always.

DOES IT SHOW A LACK OF FAITH ON THE PART OF THE CHRISTIAN TO TAKE MEDICINE?

No! Infrequent references to medication and herbal treatment in both the Old and the New Testaments make it clear that the use of remedies was not viewed as a denial of trust in the Lord. God can work through medical treatment, or He can work without it (II Ki. 20:7; I Tim. 5:23).

In fact, the Lord has healed millions of people down through the centuries in hospitals, even while under the care of a physician. If it were sin or wrong for such to be, then the Lord would be contradicting Himself by doing such.

While the Lord doesn't need the help of anyone to do anything, still, He at times definitely does use the art of medical science to aid and abet in the healing process. So, the taking of medicine or availing oneself of treatment at the hands of a physician doesn't show a lack of faith in God anymore than the believer going to church shows a lack of faith as it regards the Lord forgiving sin.

In fact, we are told that in the coming kingdom age, the Lord will provide medicine for the entirety of the world (Ezek. 47:12). This medicine will come from the leaves of the trees that will grow beside the river that will come from the new temple that will be built in Jerusalem. In fact, many, if not most medicines now come from plants, etc. So, if the taking of medicine is wrong, then God will be sinning when He does this thing in a coming day. Of course, we know that God cannot sin.

SICKNESS AND ISAIAH 53

Isaiah uses words for sickness and healing in this great passage that portrays Jesus as the suffering servant. Concerning this chapter, an argument has raged, I suppose, throughout the duration of the church, as to whether healing is in the atonement, etc. Healing is not only in the atonement but every single thing that man lost at the fall as well. While it's certainly true that we do not now have everything that Jesus purchased for us by the shedding of His own precious blood, still, we do now have everything as it pertains to salvation and victory, with the balance coming at the resurrection (Rom. 8:23).

However, healing being in the atonement no more means that no Christian will ever be sick than salvation from sin being in the atonement means that no Christian will ever again sin. Of course, salvation is most definitely in the atonement.

When Jesus went to the Cross, which is what Isaiah 53 portrays, He addressed every single thing that man lost at the fall. Absolutely nothing was excluded! However, we have to understand the atonement in the light of this particular dispensation.

Paul cleared it up very succinctly when he said: *"For we know in part, and we prophesy in part. But when that which is perfect is come* (the resurrection), *then that which is in part shall be done away .... For now we see through a glass, darkly; but then face to face: now I know in part; but then shall I know even as also I am known"* (I Cor. 13:9-10, 12). He then said:

> *Behold, I show you a mystery; We shall not all sleep, but we shall all be changed, In a moment, in the twinkling of an eye, at the last trump: for the trumpet shall sound, and the dead shall be raised incorruptible, and we shall be changed. For this corruptible must put on incorruption, and this mortal must put on immortality. So when this corruptible shall have put on*

*incorruption, and this mortal shall have put on immortality,
then shall be brought to pass the saying that is written, Death
is swallowed up in victory* (I Cor. 15:51-54).

Then there shall be no more sickness and no more dying.
What a day that will be!

The apostle also said: *"For the earnest expectation of the creature* (creation) *waits for the manifestation* (the resurrection) *of
the sons of God .... Because the creature* (creation) *itself also shall
be delivered from the bondage of corruption into the glorious liberty
of the children of God"* (Rom. 8:19, 21).

The bottom line is that we have some things now for which
Jesus paid in the atonement, which Paul refers to as the *"firstfruits
of the Spirit."* However, at the coming resurrection, we will have
everything for which He paid in the atonement (Rom. 8:23).

Even though the Lord definitely heals now in answer to
prayer, the truth is that these physical bodies are getting older
and as a result, they are wearing out. With the wearing out process comes physical afflictions and problems, which will not be
ameliorated until the redemption of the body (Rom. 8:23). As
stated, all of this will take place at the resurrection when every
saint of God at that time will receive a glorified body, which
will not be susceptible to sickness or disease in any capacity.

SICKNESS AND THE GOSPELS

The Old Testament forges direct links between sickness and God. The New Testament does not deny such a

relationship (Acts 12:23), but yet, a different emphasis emerges in the Gospels.

In the Gospels, we see a definite link between sickness and demonic powers. This is certainly not to say that all sickness is the result of such activity, but it is definitely meant to say that some sickness falls into that category, probably far more than we realize.

A typical happening is described in Luke 13:10-16. A woman, crippled for 18 years, was released from her infirmity on the Sabbath. When attacked for healing on the Sabbath, Jesus confronted his critics and said, *"Ought* (Should) *not this woman, being a daughter of Abraham, whom Satan has bound* (kept bound*), lo, these eighteen years* (for 18 long years), *be loosed from this bond on the Sabbath day?* (set free on the Sabbath day from what bound her)" (Lk. 13:16).

Her identification by Jesus as a daughter of Abraham puts her within the family of faith. This tells us that even God's people are at times bound by forces hostile to God. This also tells us that most sickness is not *caused* by God, though it may be *permitted* by Him. We have to come to the conclusion that Satan can do nothing but that God allows him to do so (Job 1-2). To believe less is to make God subservient to Satan, which is ridiculous.

SICKNESS AND DEMONIC FORCES

This theme of sickness being caused by demonic forces is actually repeated again and again in the Gospels, as in

Matthew 12. On this occasion, Jesus healed a blind mute whose disability was caused by demons. The frustrated Pharisees tried to start a rumor: Jesus must be in league with Satan to have such power over demons. However, Jesus pointed out that no divided kingdom can stand. Satan does not fight against Satan. It is the kingdom of God—the beneficent influence of God at work among humanity—to which Jesus' healings testify.

Throughout the New Testament, illness and disease are associated with the forces hostile to God and to humanity. Throughout the Gospels, Jesus is always healing, never once causing illness. While the weaknesses of humanity reflect the reality of human alienation from God, Jesus' attitude and actions show that God is and yearns to be man's healer. To see illness only as punishment is to misread the nature of God and to misunderstand the nature of those forces that distort human experience.

SICKNESS AS IT RELATES TO SIN

The link the Old Testament forged between sin and illness is not broken by the New Testament. Sin may bring divine judgment in the form of illness. Luke reports that when Herod *"gave not God the glory* (did not give praise to God)*"* when he was blasphemously honored by the people as a god, *"the* (an) *angel of the Lord smote him* (struck him down): *... And he was eaten of* (by) *worms, and gave up the ghost* (and died)*"* (Acts 12:23).

As well, Paul links the sickness of many in Corinth to their failure to discern the Lord's body when gathered for communion (I Cor. 11:27-32). This speaks of not properly understanding the Cross of Christ—what Jesus did there for us by the giving of Himself, i.e., the Lord's body.

In each of these cases, the link between personal sin and sickness is affirmed. However, the emphasis in the New Testament is on the other causes of sickness than personal sin. Sickness is an expression of the death that has passed on to humanity with our original infection by sin, brought on by the fall of Adam in the garden of Eden. In this broad sense, all sickness is linked with sin, but not every person's sickness is linked with his or her personal sin.

WHAT JESUS SAID

The disciples, like others in their time, had an erroneous concept of sin and sickness. They assumed that there was a link between sickness and personal sin in every case.

One day they pointed out a man who had been born blind and asked Jesus, *"Who did sin, this man, or his parents, that he was born blind?"* (Jn. 9:2). Jesus answered, *"Neither has this man sinned, nor his parents"* (Jn. 9:3).

Actually, Jesus wasn't saying that neither the man nor his parents had ever sinned, but rather that his affliction was not a result of personal sin at all. Rather, Jesus said, *"That the works of God should be made manifest in him"* (Jn. 9:3). Then Jesus went on to restore the man's sight (Jn. 9:6-7).

While Jesus did not go into much explanation there, the idea is that Satan had caused this thing, but whatever Satan had caused, the power of God could un-cause. In fact, that is the story of the gospel.

Consequently, as it regards individual sickness, the portrait displayed in the New Testament goes beyond that of the Old Testament. Sickness is imposed on individuals by hostile forces that delight in human suffering. Although God permits suffering, He is capable of redeeming any experience that displays itself in the physical bodies of particular Christians. He does so by His own wondrous working power.

SICKNESS AND THE MINISTRY OF
CHRIST TO THE WHOLE PERSON

Special insight into the biblical implication of health is gained when we note the manner in which Jesus did certain things.

Often Jesus' healings of physical ailments were associated with the forgiveness of sins (Mk. 2:1-12; Lk. 5:17-26). John 5 is especially suggestive. Jesus spoke to one who had been an invalid for 38 years. He first asked, *"Will you be made whole?"* (Jn. 5:6).

This man's inner self and his body were both in some sense crushed by the years of sickness. When Jesus healed him, He warned, *"Sin no more, lest a worse thing come unto you"* (Jn. 5:14). Restoration thus touched the man physically, mentally, and spiritually. The same thought is conveyed in the restoration of the prodigal son, who came back to his family, once again *"safe and sound"* (Lk. 15:27).

Even though there is clear-cut teaching about the relationship between the spiritual and the physical aspects of a person, still, the links between forgiveness and healing are very suggestive.

What is clear is that in Jesus' ministry, spirit, soul, and body are not divorced. Jesus sought always to minister to the whole person, and we might say again that he never turned one away. He never said to anyone who was sick, "I cannot heal you now because you are not living right." He never said to anyone, "You don't have enough faith." In fact, if that were the case, and it definitely was with some, Jesus gave them the faith they needed.

GOD IS THE SOURCE OF HEALTH FOR HUMANITY

The Bible views health as wellness, a condition in which a person fully exercises all of his or her capacities as a living being. Sickness is weakness—a diminishing or limiting of these capacities in the individual.

The Old Testament relates sickness in human beings to God and also to sin. But yet, we must understand sickness as it relates to God in the sense of sowing and reaping. Sickness did not and does not originate with God, with its source being Satan, i.e., sin, whether directly or indirectly.

God is the source of health for humanity. Right relationship with Him means an experience of His healing touch. Sin is the enemy of the body as well as of the spirit. However, personal sin may bring sickness as one of the many different judgments from God.

THE NEW TESTAMENT

The New Testament accepts the suppositions of the Old Testament but adds details to the picture. While sickness has sin as its original source, an individual's sickness is not necessarily related to his or her personal sin. Mankind is trapped in wreckage that is scattered across the whole earth by Adam's sin, and man is also vulnerable to the malicious attacks of demons. Even the faithful believer may be victimized by Satan. That's one of the reasons that Jesus said in the Lord's Prayer, *"Lead us not into temptation* (don't allow us to be led into temptation)*; but deliver us from evil"* (Matt. 6:13).

Similarly, God's role in sickness is expanded in the New Testament. While we have to recognize the fact that God is the cause of some sickness, His actual role is that of healer. Jesus gives us a taste of the kingdom in His healing ministry. We see sickness attacked by Jesus as an enemy, not used by Him as a scourge. This means that in the New Testament, we sense the love of God, who yearns to heal, and who only reluctantly plays judge before the time for judgment.

I think it is obvious that God permits sickness for His own good purposes, with Him using such as discipline or even judgment. Sometimes His wisdom demands such. So, we can answer the question, "Is it always God's will to heal the sick?" Yes, it is always God's will to do such, but it is not always His wisdom.

However, the role that God plays when we allow Him to do so, and I speak of obedience and faith on our part, is that of healer.

LET HIM CALL FOR THE ELDERS OF THE CHURCH

The heading refers to pastors. In Titus 1:5, 7, and Acts 20:17, 28, elders and bishops (or pastors or overseers) are equated. In Acts 20:28, the elders are instructed to shepherd the church of God, that is, to do the work of an overseer or pastor. That elder, bishop, and pastor refer to the same office is also suggested in I Peter 5:1-4. This means that the names or titles—pastor, elder, bishop, overseer, and presbyter—all refer, without exception, to the pastor of a local church.

Unfortunately, the church has attempted to take one or more of these titles, such as bishop, and make more of it than does the Scripture. In other words, by doing such, they have changed the government of the church and instituted that which the Holy Spirit has never sanctioned. To say it another way: These particular higher offices are purely of man's invention and actually began in the second century. It finally evolved into what we presently know as the Catholic Church; however, the Protestants have been guilty of the same sin.

As well, even though James did not mention it, prayer for the sick can be offered by any believer. The Scripture plainly says, *"These signs shall follow them who believe"* (Mk. 16:17-18).

AND LET THEM PRAY OVER HIM

The heading refers to asking the Lord for healing regarding the need. While the anointing with oil is very important, as we shall see, prayer is the more significant of the two ministries performed by the elders. The word *pray* is the main verb, while the word *anoint* is a participle. As well, the overall emphasis of the paragraph is on prayer. So, the anointing, although very important, is a secondary action.

From the entirety of the teaching on prayer as it regards the Word of God, we must understand that prayer is a privilege and not merely a duty. In fact, if it is looked at as a duty, we completely miss the importance of what this is all about. The idea presented here is that we are to ask the Lord for healing, or whatever is needed, that He will hear our petition, and that He will answer. Now, the question for you, the reader, is this: Do you believe that?

I realize that we would think that all Christians should believe that, as they certainly should; however, due to false teaching behind the pulpit, unbelief is rampant. In other words, a lot of so-called Christians simply don't believe that God hears and answers prayer.

It is my belief that much of the doubt expressed by many comes from the fact that they are not Spirit-filled. If such comes from one who claims to be Spirit-filled, to deny the effectiveness of prayer certainly means that they are not Spirit-led. One of the first things that happens to the Spirit-filled believer is that he begins to look to God who hears and answers prayers. He begins to believe that God is able to do all things, in other words, a God of might and miracles.

My hope is built on nothing less
Than Jesus' blood and righteousness,
I will not trust the sweetest frame,
But wholly lean, on Jesus' name.

On Christ the solid rock I stand,
All other ground is sinking sand,
All other ground is sinking sand.

DIVINE *Healing*

CHAPTER 7

ANOINTING HIM WITH OIL

ANOINTING HIM WITH OIL

THE PHRASE, "ANOINTING HIM with oil" presents an act that is commanded by the Holy Spirit. It has no medicinal purposes as some claim.

This anointing is symbolic of the healing of God by the Holy Spirit. In fact, the Holy Spirit is symbolized in several ways:

- *Water* (Jn. 7:38-39). Water is a symbol of life.
- *Fire* (Mat. 3:11). Fire symbolizes purity.
- *Wind* (Acts 2:2). Wind symbolizes power.
- *Dove* (Jn. 1:32). The dove symbolizes gentleness.
- *Oil* (James 5:14). Oil symbolizes healing.

Even though the anointing with oil is not absolutely required as it regards praying for the sick, etc., it is helpful because it is symbolic of healing. As well, it provides a point of contact for the one for whom prayer is being offered. When Jesus sent out the Twelve, the Scripture says, *"They cast out many devils* (demons)*, and anointed with oil many who were sick, and healed them"* (Mk. 6:7-13). Even though the Scripture doesn't plainly say, it is certain that Jesus told them to do this. And yet, the Scripture tells us that many were healed in Jerusalem simply by the shadow of Peter passing over them as he passed by. No anointing with oil was used in this case (Acts 5:15-16).

IN THE NAME OF THE LORD

The heading presents where the real power resides.

Saints of God have the privilege of using the name of Jesus (Mk. 16:17). This comes under the heading of the "authority of the believer." However, such authority is always exercised in the spirit world and never over other people (Eph. 6:10-12).

It should be noted, as well, that the use of the name of Jesus is not a magic talisman that automatically causes devils to tremble, etc. To be sure, it carries power in the spirit world that is beyond our comprehension, but yet, it must be understood according to the following: I think it is proper to say that the power of Christ as God did not at all diminish in His incarnation. While He then functioned as a man and not God, still, He was anointed and helped by the Holy Spirit more so than any human being has ever known (Ps. 45:7).

The point I'm attempting to make is that His power was almighty before the incarnation, was almighty during the incarnation, and continues to be almighty at present and will be forever. So, the name of Jesus, or *"the name of the Lord,"* as James used the term, must carry a special significance other than the mere fact of Him being Lord.

We as believers are given the ability and privilege of using the name of Jesus because of the Cross. When Jesus died on the Cross, He not only satisfied the demands of the broken law, He also totally defeated Satan and all the cohorts of darkness. By satisfying the demands of the broken law, in essence, He satisfied the demands of God. By the doing of that, He atoned for all sin. In other words, by His death on the Cross, which included the pouring out of His precious blood, He destroyed any legal right that Satan had as it regarded holding humanity captive. Satan's legal right is sin, and with sin removed, which it was at the Cross, the Evil One lost that legal right, at least for those who will believe (Jn. 3:16).

Whenever the believing sinner comes to Christ, which he does by faith, he is literally placed in Christ. This place and position is attained through the crucifixion. In other words, we were literally baptized into His death, which has no reference whatsoever to water baptism, but it actually refers to the crucifixion of Christ (Rom. 6:3).

FAITH

Naturally, we were not there when all of this happened; however, simple faith in Christ and what He did for us at the Cross places us there in the mind of God. Inasmuch as we are in Christ (Rom. 6:3-14; 8:1-2), we now have the privilege of using His name.

In the privilege of using that name, which we do by faith, the believer must understand that the Cross is what made it all possible. When the believer understands that, which means that his faith is in what Christ did at the Cross, the Holy Spirit will then back up the use of that name (Rom. 8:2, 11).

Many Christians use the name of Jesus without much success. It confuses them because they expect more. Let me explain: When Satan attacks the child of God, most Christians have been taught to use the name of Jesus against him. Many are somewhat disillusioned when they use the name, and nothing seems to happen. In other words, Satan doesn't exactly break and run. The reason is simple, yet, elusive—just as the Word of God is not a magic talisman, neither is the name of Jesus. By that, I mean the mere quoting of the Word or the name does not work any magic powers in the spirit world.

THE REASON FOR THE POWER

However, if the Christian knows and understands what is behind the name, or rather what makes it possible for us to use the name, and I continue to speak of the Cross, then the name of Jesus will take on a brand-new meaning. Satan knows if your faith is in the Cross or something else. Regrettably, the faith of most Christians is not in the Cross simply because they know very little about the Cross. As a result, there is no power in what they do, which Satan readily recognizes.

While the power is in the Holy Spirit (Acts 1:8), the Spirit functions totally and completely within the parameters of the finished work of Christ. Consequently, He demands faith in that finished work. With that being the case, the use of the name of Jesus becomes a power of unprecedented proportions. To be sure, Satan will then recognize the use of that name under those auspices (Rom. 8:2).

"And the prayer of faith shall save the sick, and the Lord shall raise him up; and if he have committed sins, they shall be forgiven him" (James 5:15).

AND THE PRAYER OF FAITH SHALL SAVE THE SICK

The heading presents a beautiful promise.

What is the prayer of faith?

It is simply the belief that God hears and answers prayer.

This of which James speaks doesn't actually include the gift of faith, the gifts of healing, or working of miracles (I Cor. 12:9-10). Those are in a category all to themselves. This of which James speaks applies to any preacher of the gospel (called the elders), or actually any believer (Mk. 16:17-18). It is the simple matter of believing God and His Word.

WHAT DOES THE PRAYER OF FAITH GUARANTEE?

The automatic response to that is that it guarantees healing; however, if that were the case, that would make God subject to our faith when the truth is that our faith is subject to God.

The meaning is that if the person is healed, and some are, it will be the Lord honoring the prayer of faith to bring about such.

Many have misunderstood this passage, thereby, claiming that if the person is not healed, that means the prayer of faith hasn't been prayed. Oftentimes, we will hear Christians say, "I want somebody to pray the prayer of faith over me."

While that is certainly a legitimate desire, it should be understood that someone praying the prayer of faith doesn't exactly mean that the desired results will be brought about. Let us state it again: Every single promise in the Word of God is subject to the will and wisdom of God.

GOD'S WILL IS NEVER SUBJECT TO OUR FAITH

While I personally believe that it's always the will of God to heal the sick, there may definitely be times when it is not His wisdom to do so. We cannot take faith and force God into an action that is not what He wants and desires. As stated, our faith is always subject to His will, but His will is never subject to our faith. Unfortunately, many in the modern church have been taught that He is, in fact, subject to our faith.

There are many Christians who think in their hearts and minds, "If I only had enough faith, I could …"

No! That's not the case at all. God is not sitting up in heaven measuring our faith, and if it rises to a certain level, then He will be moved to do certain things. Actually, it's not quantity of faith that is needed, but rather the quality of faith. What do we mean by that?

Once again we go back to the Cross. For our faith to be properly anchored in the Word of God, we must have it anchored in the Cross. Considering that the Cross is what makes it possible for God to deal with man, and for that matter, for man to deal with God, the Cross is where our faith must be anchored. Of course, the Cross of Christ was always and will ever be the will of God.

AND THE LORD SHALL RAISE HIM UP

As is obvious, the heading proclaims the Lord as the healer.

Divine healing is very, very special to me personally. I was wondrously and gloriously healed by the Lord at about 10 years of age. Perhaps this short testimony would be of benefit and blessing to you. I have already given an account of my healing at the first part of this book, so I won't go through the entirety of the testimony again but only so much as to make the points I wish to make.

The year was 1945. The doctors could not find out what was wrong with me. They ruled out malaria plus several other things. I stayed nauseous almost constantly and would go unconscious at times.

Actually, this happened (unconsciousness) several times at school, with my parents having to go get me. The last time it took place, it became very personal to all concerned.

After one such episode, my parents picked me up, and the school principal told them that if something was not done for me, they were going to have to take me out of school. The principal said, "We don't want him dying on our hands." That's how bad the situation was.

As stated, the doctors ruled out about everything that one could think. I personally believe that it was Satan trying to kill me. He knew that God would use me to touch this world for Christ, and he was doing all that he could to stop it, but thank God, he didn't succeed.

The day that I received healing was a Sunday. Service had ended in our little church, and my parents were to take the pastor and his wife to lunch, which they did. However, we first had to stop and pray for a parishioner.

When that was done, we were all standing in the front room when my dad said, "Brother Culbreth (that was the pastor's name), please anoint Jimmy with oil and pray for him again."

Now, understand that this pastor, along with scores of people in our small church, had already prayed for me several times in the past months, but seemingly, all to no avail. In other words, I was as sick as ever, if not sicker.

However, that particular Sunday afternoon at about 1:30 p.m., the pastor walked across the floor, put some oil on his finger from the small bottle he was holding, and touched my head. The moment that he did it, it was something like a ball of fire about the size of a softball that started at the top of my head and slowly went down my body, down both legs, and out my feet.

I instantly knew that I was healed. While I felt the heat spread through my body, it did not burn but only had the sensation of heat. No one had to tell me that I was healed—I knew that I was. To be sure, I have not suffered anything of that nature from that day until this. Actually, for the most part,

I have enjoyed miraculous health. Today, at 83 years of age, I've never felt better, and, of course, we give the Lord all the praise and all the glory.

GREAT TRUTHS

First of all, I'm so glad that my parents attended a church where the pastor believed in healing.

It was very small, and as far as most people were concerned, it was of little significance. However, this pastor and most of the few people who attended this little assembly were godly, and that's all that mattered. Had my parents attended a church that didn't believe in divine healing, I don't really believe I would be alive today.

Second, I'm glad my parents didn't quit praying for me after not seeing any success the first time, or even after several times. Had they stopped, again, I don't believe I would be alive today.

While we do not have the answers to many questions concerning situations of this nature, we do know that God does everything for a reason, and He does everything well. I do believe that He tests our faith. It's in the testing of our faith that many of us fail—we quit, we lose heart, and we allow doubt to come in.

The Scripture plainly says: *"But without faith it is impossible to please Him: for he who comes to God must believe that He is, and that He is a rewarder of them who diligently seek Him"* (Heb. 11:6).

AND IF HE HAVE COMMITTED SINS, THEY SHALL BE FORGIVEN HIM

The heading tells us two things:

1. The conditional clause, *"if he have sinned,"* makes it clear that not all sickness is the result of sin.
2. If, in fact, the sickness has been caused by sin, which is directly or indirectly the case more often than we realize, not only will the Lord heal but, as well, will also forgive the sin. This is paralleled in the ministry of Christ.

The Scripture says, *"And they come unto Him, bringing one sick of the palsy, which was borne of four."* It then said, *"When Jesus saw their faith, He said unto the sick of the palsy, Son, your sins be forgiven you"* (Mk. 2:3, 5).

Evidently, this man's sickness had been caused in some way by sin. When we say that, we are speaking of something the man had personally done or a particular lifestyle in which he had engaged that was wrong.

As it regarded the healing and forgiveness, Jesus linked them both together. He said: *"Whether is it easier to say to the sick of the palsy, Your sins be forgiven you; or to say, Arise, and take up your bed, and walk?"* (Mk. 2:9). The same power that was needed for one was needed for the other.

A DILEMMA

So, what are we saying? We are saying that man is in a terrible dilemma, and the harder he tries within his own means to extricate himself from this dilemma, the worse it seems to become. However, man has recourse in Christ, and man has recourse only in Christ. Jesus paid a terrible price that we might be lifted out of this morass of sin, sickness, and evil of every nature. That price was the shedding of His own blood on the Cross, which was done on our behalf.

All of this—the healing and the forgiveness—speaks of grace. As is known, grace is the goodness of God extended to undeserving believers. In fact, no believer is deserving, and herein lies the great problem.

At times we seem to think as believers that we are deserving; consequently, we think in our hearts that the Lord owes us healing or something of this nature. He doesn't! He owes us nothing!

Accordingly, we must come to the place that we know and realize this before we can actually receive from the Lord. This speaks of humility. I firmly believe that the prayer of faith is closely tied to brokenness and humility, and again I stress that such can be obtained only by a proper interpretation of the Cross.

"Confess your faults one to another, and pray one for another, that you may be healed. The effectual fervent prayer of a righteous man avails much" (James 5:16).

CONFESS YOUR FAULTS ONE TO ANOTHER

The heading refers to being quick to admit fault if such be the case. It's very difficult for some Christians to simply say,

"I am wrong," and it is Christians to whom James speaks. Far too often, Christians try to lay the blame of their wrongdoing on others.

In the Greek, the word *fault* is *paraptoma,* and it means "a falling aside when one should have stood upright; a transgression; a moral fall."

In all of this, the idea is presented that if we do not take personal blame, at least when we are at fault, such a position will definitely hinder our prayers from being answered, if not stop the answers altogether. James is speaking here of accepting responsibility; however, what does that mean?

ACCEPTING RESPONSIBILITY

It's very simple. It means that we are to admit our fault, ask forgiveness of the ones we have wronged, and, of course, also confess our sin to the Lord (I Jn. 1:9).

We are to then understand that the reason for our wrongdoing is because we have moved our faith from the Cross of Christ, which guarantees us the help of the Holy Spirit, to something else, which guarantees failure. In effect, we are to come back to the Cross.

However, accepting responsibility has a far different meaning with most Christians. The reason is that most Christians function under law instead of grace. Accepting responsibility to most Christians refers to the individual who has done wrong submitting to men, whomever those men might be, and then doing whatever they demand to be done, irrespective of how unscriptural it might be. That is what is referred to in the majority of the church as accepting responsibility.

The truth is that such a course is the sure road to spiritual disaster. In fact, most of the time, those who follow such a course make no claims at all as it regards whether or not their position is scriptural. In other words, the Bible plays no part whatsoever in their actions, and in truth, they don't even really claim that it does. They just make up the rules as they go along, and whatever those rules are, they demand that they be followed. If the person refuses to follow these unscriptural rules, he is branded as being in rebellion. Then he is fair game for anything.

THE CROSS OF CHRIST

In such a situation, which, in fact, is predominant, it doesn't matter at all that the individual in question has earnestly sought God for forgiveness and, in fact, has been forgiven. Not adhering to the Word of God, those things play no part in the thinking of most so-called religious leaders.

So, when the Holy Spirit through James tells us here to confess our faults, it carries little weight in most modern religious circles. That is tragic but true! However, if we will confess our faults, forgiveness by the Lord will always be enjoined.

There is only one answer for sin, and it doesn't matter who commits the sin, and that is the Cross of Christ. That is where sin was addressed and defeated. Consequently, at the Cross the guilt of sin was removed, and its power was broken. All that is required is for the person to have faith in that which Christ has done for us (Rom. 5:1). So, the entirety of the situation boils down to accepting what Christ has done or demanding something else. In fact, this is not new, having begun at the very dawn of time.

God told the first family that the sacrifice of an innocent victim (a lamb) was the only means by which sin could be atoned and fellowship with God restored and maintained (Gen. 4). Abel believed that and was accepted by God (Gen. 4:4). Cain brought another type of offering, which God would not accept (Gen. 4:5-7). That was the problem then, has continued to be the problem through the centuries, and is the problem now. Do we accept what Christ has done, or do we attempt to add things to what He has done?

THE QUESTION

Many argue that this is not the question at all; however, if it's not the question, then what is the question? No, that is the question. Either the blood of Jesus Christ, God's Son, cleanses us from all sin, or else, it doesn't (I Jn. 1:7). We cannot have it both ways. If it does, then we don't need to look to other things. Also, if we try to add other things, we invalidate the cleansing effect.

A TESTIMONY

Many years ago, something happened in a particular church that pretty well explains what we are addressing.

A young man in the church, who happened to be the pastor's son, fell in love with a young lady in the church, and they proposed marriage.

The situation caused a tremendous rupture in the church, which threatened to split it, etc.

Why?

The young lady in question, who had a tremendous experience with Christ and was now living a dedicated life that was obvious to all, had formerly been a prostitute before she gave her heart to Christ. With the church knowing this, the split ensued. Some stated that they would not have their pastor's son marry someone of this nature. As stated, the situation was quickly going from bad to worse.

On a particular Sunday morning at the very height of the terrible controversy, a dear lady, aged in years, stood to her feet and asked if she could say a word. The pastor gladly consented, knowing her life and walk with the Lord were impeccable.

As the audience grew quiet with every eye fastened on her, she began to speak.

She said, "I have watched this situation as it has developed, actually threatening the future of the church. We all know the young lady in question, that her life is impeccable, and she has had a tremendous experience with the Lord. No one can deny that."

And then she said, "In reality, it's not the young man who wants to marry this young lady who is on trial, and neither is it the young lady as it regards her life and living before coming to Christ that is on trial. What is on trial here is the precious shed blood of the Lord Jesus Christ. Does the blood of Jesus cleanse from all sin, or does it not cleanse?"

A silence filled the building. You could have heard the proverbial pin drop. In a few moments' time, the entirety of the church knew they had heard the truth. In fact, it was the blood of Christ that was on trial, and those who had felt that the young lady was not good enough to marry the pastor's son suddenly realized the wickedness of their thinking.

Every believer should understand that the child of God has no past, and we might quickly add, the Devil has no future.

AND PRAY ONE FOR ANOTHER, THAT YOU MAY BE HEALED

The heading tells us two things:

1. If we have wronged someone, and we refuse to confess our fault to the one we have wronged, we can forget about prayer for healing.

2. If we have, in fact, sinned by wronging someone, and we properly confess our fault to him, the way is then opened back up for our prayers to be heard by the Lord and for Him to answer.

God doesn't demand perfection from saints. If He did, where would any of us be? However, He does demand that we have faith in Christ and what He did at the Cross on our behalf and, in fact, that we continue to do that all the days of our lives. If such is done, the Holy Spirit will help us as only He can do (Rom. 8:11). Several things will then happen:

- Sin will not have dominion over us (Rom. 6:14).
- A constant looking to the Cross (Lk. 9:23) will develop humility in the heart and life of the believer, who will be quick to confess a fault if, in fact, such has been committed. The Cross demands that.
- The only place of victory for the child of God is faith in the Cross of Christ, which guarantees the help of the Spirit (I Cor. 1:18).

All healing is found in what Jesus did at the Cross. Peter plainly said: *"Who His own self bear our sins in His own body on the tree* (Cross)*, that we, being dead to sins* (due to having been crucified with Him [Rom. 6:3])*, should live unto righteousness* (by having continued faith in what Christ did at the Cross)*: by whose stripes you were healed"* (I Pet. 2:24).

THE EFFECTUAL FERVENT PRAYER OF
A RIGHTEOUS MAN AVAILS MUCH

The heading presents several things about this that we should note:
- First of all, the Holy Spirit is the one who said this through James, which means that it is perfectly valid.
- The righteousness here addressed is that which is given freely by God upon one's faith in Christ and what He did at the Cross, and which shows itself in righteous works.
- Prayer from such a source avails much.

However, this is so important that we need to look at it a little more closely: First of all, we must define righteousness.

The simple fact is that much prayer is coming from many Christians that stems from self-righteousness rather than the righteousness of God. There is an addendum to that: Due to the fact that such prayers are never answered, there simply isn't much praying in the church at the present. This that James tells us is really the reason.

TRUE RIGHTEOUSNESS

Let's see what true righteousness actually is: God has always had righteousness and, in fact, is righteousness. As a definition, righteousness is simply that which is right; however, the definition of what is right is that which is given by God and not by man. That definition in totality is the Word of God.

At the same time, fallen man, and that includes all, has no righteousness (the Scripture plainly says, *"There is none righteous, no, not one"* [Rom. 3:10]).

RIGHTEOUSNESS TO SINFUL MAN

So, the great question was, How does God transfer His righteousness to sinful man? Of course, with God being God, there may have been many other ways that such a thing could be done; however, the way that He chose was by becoming man Himself and paying the price that must be paid in order for this work to be accomplished (I Pet. 1:18-20). I might add that He actually chose the way before the foundation of the world, in other words, before man was ever created. The price was high!

It would require His taking of the penalty of sin for every human being, and that penalty was death. In other words, the very reason that God would become man was that He might die on the Cross, thereby, satisfying this terrible sin debt.

In His life, Jesus kept the law perfectly in every respect, which, of course, was an absolute necessity inasmuch as He was our substitute. However, that within itself would not redeem anyone. The penalty for man's terrible crime had to be paid, and, as stated, that penalty was death (Rom. 6:23).

When Jesus died on the Cross, thereby, shedding His life's blood and satisfying the claims of the broken law, God the Father accepted the payment. What did that mean?

That meant that for anyone who would register faith in Christ, God would award such an individual the perfect righteousness of God. To register faith in Christ means that a person accepts God's verdict of guilty about himself and God's verdict about Christ—that His payment is accepted. It's called imputed righteousness, which means that it is righteousness awarded as a free gift.

THE GIFT OF RIGHTEOUSNESS

Paul said, *"For if by one man's offence* (Adam) *death reigned by one; much more they which receive abundance of grace and of the gift of righteousness shall reign in life by one, Jesus Christ"* (Rom. 5:17).

As plainly stated, it is the gift of righteousness, which actually refers to imputed righteousness.

This is the only type of righteousness that God will accept. If we try to present to Him any other type of righteousness, God will not accept it at all. By that, I speak of something that we think we've earned or goodness that we think we have attained by our good works, etc.

So, when someone accepts totally and freely what Christ has done for him at the Cross, that man is looked at by God as righteous because the righteousness he has is the righteousness of God. This refers to that for which Christ paid the price at the Cross and not righteousness of his own making. God will heed the prayer of such a person, but only such a person.

ELIJAH WAS A MAN SUBJECT TO LIKE PASSIONS AS WE ARE

"Elijah was a man subject to like passions as we are, and he prayed earnestly that it might not rain: and it rained not on the earth by the space of three years and six months. And he prayed again, and the heaven gave rain, and the earth brought forth her fruit" (James 5:17-18).

The Holy Spirit gives this example because He wants us to know that what is in the reach of one is in the reach of the other.

James is illustrating the effectiveness of prayer. In doing this, he refers to an undoubted case where prayer had such effectiveness. However, this might be objected to on the grounds that Elijah was a distinguished prophet, and it was reasonable to suppose that his prayer would be heard.

It might even be said that his example could not be used to prove that the prayers of those who were not favored with such advantages would be heard.

To meet this, the apostle said that Elijah was a mere man, and that, therefore, his case is one that should encourage all to pray. He was no superhuman. In fact, immediately after the prayer of verse 18 was answered, which was a tremendous miracle, this very prophet grew so discouraged that he even prayed to God that he might die (I Ki. 19:4).

We have a tendency to think of these prophets of old and the apostles of the New Testament as being superhuman. To counter that erroneous direction, the Holy Spirit picked one of the greatest prophets of all, Elijah, to serve as an example of what He was saying.

SO WHAT IS THE LESSON HE WANTS US TO LEARN?

These men didn't see great things done for God because they were of a different fiber than we are. In fact, they were all of the same family of frail humanity—men of like passions with us—but this is what made the difference: Despite their frailty, these men dared to believe God, and, as well, they gave to Him full control of their lives.

Because of erroneous teaching, we as Christians, I think, little understand faith, or righteousness for that matter. Thinking of either one, faith or righteousness, we look to ourselves, which is the wrong place to look. It's the source of faith and righteousness that makes the difference. Of course, that source is Christ, and more particularly, what He did for us at the Cross. This is the story of the Bible and, in fact, the total story of the Bible. We know that *"faith comes by hearing, and hearing by the Word of God"* (Rom. 10:17), and we also know, as stated, that the Bible is the story of man's redemption.

The problem is that we make ourselves the source of faith and righteousness, which is backward. The source, as stated, must be Christ and Him crucified (I Cor. 2:2).

As well, we sometimes think that faith and righteousness are attributes that we can use as we choose. That is not the case at all. These men and women of God outlined in the Bible who performed great things for the Lord were doing what God wanted them to do. Faith will only function in this capacity.

AND HE PRAYED EARNESTLY THAT IT MIGHT NOT RAIN: AND IT RAINED NOT ON THE EARTH BY THE SPACE OF THREE YEARS AND SIX MONTHS

The heading refers to the apostle here using a part for the whole. Even though it uses the word *earth,* it is not speaking of the entirety of the earth, but rather that part of which it speaks, which was the northern kingdom of Israel. It was that part of the earth of which he spoke.

The Bible doesn't exactly record that Elijah prayed concerning this thing; however, neither does it say in the I Kings 17 account that he didn't. Of course, considering what the Holy Spirit said in James, we know that Elijah did pray as it regarded this matter.

There is a side issue here that we must address as well: The strength of a nation is those who know how to pray, which means that they know God. As Elijah was able to change events in Israel, events can be changed according to the will of God in any country by individuals who truly know God. In fact, the most powerful weapon on earth is faith-filled prayer, but despite all the talk about prayer, the truth is that there is actually very little praying at present in the modern church. By the erroneous teaching of false faith for the last several decades, the modern church has almost been destroyed, at least as it regards the single most important aspect of the Christian experience. It hasn't been faith in the Cross that has been taught, but rather faith in something else altogether. If it's not faith in the Cross, then it's not faith that God will recognize (Rom. 5:1-2).

AND HE PRAYED AGAIN

The heading presents the prophet asking the Lord now to change what had been done. Three and one-half years earlier he had prayed that the rain would stop, and now he prays that it will once again come upon the earth.

In the midst of all of this, God was showing Israel something. The physical drought was a portrayal of their spiritual condition. The gathering of the people at Mount Carmel, with Elijah repairing *"the altar of the Lord that was broken down,"* portrays the Cross (I Ki. 18:30). The bullock laid on the altar and then the fire falling, which must have been a spectacular sight, was a portrayal of what Jesus would do at

Calvary when He took the judgment of God upon Himself that should have come upon us (I Ki. 18:38).

Elijah praying and the rain then coming after some three and half years was a type of the Holy Spirit coming back to a spiritually parched area (I Ki. 18:41-46).

Unfortunately, it didn't turn out that way in Israel. Nevertheless, the Lord, in effect, was telling Israel that as the rain came and restored the land, He could likewise restore the people spiritually if they would only believe Him. Unfortunately, they little responded!

AND THE HEAVEN GAVE RAIN AND THE EARTH BROUGHT FORTH HER FRUIT

The heading refers to the effect of one man's prayers. This is the power of prayer that comes from a consecrated heart and prayer that is prayed in the will of God.

I don't know how much the people of Israel knew and understood what was behind all of these events; likewise, it is for sure that the world doesn't know the cause of most events presently. However, I think I can say with scriptural and spiritual authority that many of the events that transpire on the earth presently, whether negative or positive, are influenced greatly by prayer. When one considers that the number of individuals in this world whom God can use in this manner, which, no doubt, is very small, we are then made to realize not how great and wonderful these individuals are, whomever they might be, but how great and wonderful that God is.

That's the reason I implore everyone who reads this book, who truly loves God and truly believes that God hears and answers prayer, to pray for us. I earnestly solicit your prayers because I earnestly need your prayers. Pray that God will help me to ever do His will and to finish this course of world evangelism, the responsibility of which (at least our part of that responsibility) He has given to us.

So, as it regards divine healing, we are to understand that God still answers prayer. We are to understand that He still heals. Consequently, we should earnestly seek His face and do so constantly as it regards our needs and especially divine healing.

While there aren't any divine healers as it regards men, there is a divine healer, and His name is the Lord Jesus Christ.

Our times are in Thy hand:
O God, we wish them there:
Our lives, our souls, our all, we leave
Entirely to Thy care.

Our times are in Thy hand:
Whatever they may be:
Pleasing or painful, dark or bright,
As best may seem to Thee.

Our times are in Thy hand:
Why should we doubt or fear?
A Father's hand will never cause
His child a needless tear.

Our times are in Thy hand:
Jesus the Crucified,
Whose hand our many sins have pierced,
Is now our guard and guide.

Our times are in Thy hand:
We'll always trust to Thee,
Till we possess the promised land,
And all Thy glory see.

REFERENCES

CHAPTER 2

Spence-Jones, H. D. M., ed. *The Pulpit Commentary: Numbers.* London; New York: Funk & Wagnalls Company, 1910.

CHAPTER 3

Spence, H. D. M. *The Pulpit Commentary: Mark 5:40.* Grand Rapids: Eerdmans Publishing Company, 1978.

CHAPTER 4

Wuest, Kenneth S. *Wuest's Word Studies in the Greek New Testament*: *Mark.* Grand Rapids: Eerdmans Publishing Company, 1942

Williams, George. *William's Complete Bible Commentary.* Grand Rapids: Kregel Publications, Pg. 735.

ABOUT EVANGELIST JIMMY SWAGGART

The Rev. Jimmy Swaggart is a Pentecostal evangelist whose anointed preaching and teaching has drawn multitudes to the Cross of Christ since 1955.

As an author, he has written more than 50 books, commentaries, study guides, and The Expositor's Study Bible, which has sold more than 4 million copies.

As an award-winning musician and singer, Brother Swaggart has recorded more than 50 gospel albums and sold nearly 17 million recordings worldwide.

For more than six decades, Brother Swaggart has channeled his preaching and music ministry through multiple media venues including print, radio, television and the Internet.

In 2010, Jimmy Swaggart Ministries launched its own cable channel, SonLife Broadcasting Network, which airs 24 hours a day to a potential viewing audience of more than 2 billion people around the globe.

Brother Swaggart also pastors Family Worship Center in Baton Rouge, Louisiana, the church home and headquarters of Jimmy Swaggart Ministries.

Jimmy Swaggart Ministries materials can be found at **www.jsm.org**.

ALSO BY EVANGELIST
JIMMY SWAGGART

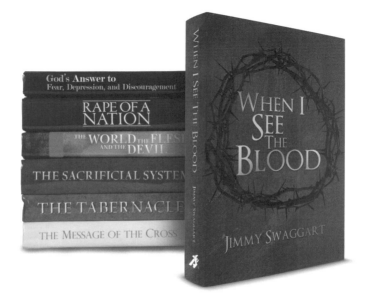

(09-122)   THE MESSAGE OF THE CROSS
(09-125)   THE TABERNACLE
(09-126)   THE SACRIFICIAL SYSTEM
(09-130)   THE WORLD, THE FLESH, AND THE DEVIL
(09-131)   RAPE OF A NATION
(09-132)   WHEN I SEE THE BLOOD
(09-133)   GOD'S ANSWER TO FEAR, DEPRESSION, AND DISCOURAGEMENT

AVAILABLE AT SHOPJSM.ORG